D1009714

A
SURVIVOR'S
JOURNEY

A
SURVIVOR'S
JOURNEY

FROM VICTIM TO ADVOCATE

Natasha Simone Alexenko

amazonpublishing

Text copyright © 2018 by Natasha Simone Alexenko
All rights reserved.

The events expressed in this book, while true, were composed from the author's
memory.

No part of this book may be reproduced, or stored in a retrieval system, or
transmitted in any form or by any means, electronic, mechanical, photocopying,
recording, or otherwise, without express written permission of the publisher.

Published by Amazon Publishing, Seattle

www.apub.com

Amazon, the Amazon logo, and Amazon Publishing are trademarks of Amazon.com,
Inc., or its affiliates.

ISBN-13: 9781503943414
ISBN-10: 1503943410

Cover design by Faceout Studio

Printed in the United States of America

*To Kim and Vish for bringing magic back into my life,
and to Brooke and Pete for reminding me to
laugh at myself.*

CONTENTS

A
SURVIVOR'S
JOURNEY

PREFACE

At its core, this is a story about love.

Perhaps you find it difficult to grasp how a story about a brutal rape could be about love. I assure you, it is. Follow me on this journey and you'll see why.

I was raped. I survived. I'm not sure that I would have, if not for the compassion of and care from family and friends, and those that I have met since that terrible night in 1993.

This is not just my story but the story of those who have been raped or known someone who's been raped. The odds are good, or, rather, bad, that you are one of these people—every one and a half minutes, an American is sexually assaulted.[1] Yet it is also the story of one horrible act of violence being drained of its power through love and compassion. It is the story of how words and actions can change the world.

It breaks my heart to know that I am the exception and not the rule. There are so many survivors of sexual assault across the globe who have not been met with kindness, who have been dismissed or ignored or, at worst, blamed or even punished for the crime committed against them. I think about those women and men, girls and boys, every day. They are the ones who drive us to show up, to go to work no matter

---

1. "Scope of the Problem: Statistics," RAINN, accessed July 6, 2017, https://www.rainn.org/statistics.

how high the mountain we have to climb, no matter how much it seems the odds are stacked against us.

It's absolutely essential that I make it clear that, though you and I might have some similarities in our experiences, I will never understand what it's like to walk in the shoes of another. Know that I recognize our differences and that my heart and mind are open to better understanding how circumstance, religion, belief, class, and race make the story of survival different for each of us.

I believe that there is no one correct way to feel about assault or talk about assault. If you've been assaulted, it's totally OK to never talk about it. It is your life, your body, and it's up to you. There is no right or wrong—there is only choice. My goal in writing this book is to share my story in the hopes that I can help to shift the paradigm of how survivors of sex crimes are treated. As you might imagine, this book was a challenge for me to write. Sometimes I have a great deal to say; other times I don't. Often it's difficult for me to share; sometimes I feel like if I don't say something I'll scream. This is a subject that touches so many of us—and all in a different way.

I have met so many amazing people through this work, and these pages are filled with their stories—their hopes and their tears. I write for each of you—those I know and those of you I don't—in every single word of this journey. You humble and inspire me.

No matter what, I acknowledge your truth. I believe you.

1.

Despite Fear

"Always wear clean underwear."
—Mom

I was raped at gunpoint just after midnight on Friday, August 6, 1993, in New York City's Upper West Side. I was twenty years old, at college in the city I'd dreamed about living in all of my life. The excruciating experience on that brutally hot, sticky night was followed by another one almost as traumatic: the rape exam.

As I lay trembling on the cold examination table, with my feet up in stirrups while the medical examiner poked, prodded, combed, snipped, and scrutinized my genitalia for clues to my abductor, I assumed my rape kit would be tested immediately. Why else would I endure such a painful, invasive, and embarrassing exam? So that law enforcement could find and put away the monster that had violated me, of course. Truthfully, I would've done just about anything they asked. I trusted law enforcement to follow through. I didn't know that it wasn't so simple.

Instead of being processed, my rape kit collected dust on the shelves of a New York County storage facility, along with 17,000 others, for nearly a decade.[2] Some estimate that the nationwide backlog of untested rape kits numbers in the hundreds of thousands, which makes sense considering that an average of one in five women in the United States reports a rape during her lifetime.[3]

I didn't know it at the time, but my former life ended that grim evening of my rape, and a new one began, one that would eventually lead to my advocacy work for rape victim justice. This would become my singular career focus, and I would go on to create Natasha's Justice Project, a national nonprofit organization dedicated to getting the nation's backlog of untested sexual assault evidence kits processed—and thereby getting more rapists off the streets.

On Thursday, September 10, 2015, twenty-two years after my rape, Natasha's Justice Project hit a significant milestone. I was once again in New York City, this time speaking on behalf of rape victims nationwide at a highly publicized press conference with Vice President Joe Biden, US Attorney General Loretta Lynch, and New York County District Attorney Cyrus Vance Jr. The trio would be announcing a significant joint effort: a pledge of nearly $80 million to be issued as grants from the New York County District Attorney's Office and the US

---

2. Maria Caspani, "Manhattan DA announces $35 mln funding for rape kit backlog," Reuters, November 12, 2014, http://www.reuters.com/article/us-new-york-sexcrimes-idUSKCN0IW2KJ20141112.

3. National Center for Injury Prevention and Control: Division of Violence Prevention, *Sexual Violence Facts at a Glance*, accessed July 6, 2017, https://www.cdc.gov/violenceprevention/pdf/sv-datasheet-a.pdf.

Department of Justice. The funding would be split between nearly fifty police agencies across the United States to pay for crime-lab processing of 70,000 untested rape kits, expediting a process to identify perpetrators of sex crimes.[4]

District Attorney Vance noted that the combined grants represented "the single largest contribution toward ending the rape kit backlog that has ever been made" and said the funding "represent[s] the best opportunity in a generation to take rapists out of our communities." He'd played an integral part in the backlog movement, and New York City had become the nation's first major metropolitan area to clear its own backlog of untested rape kits. This goal had been accomplished a decade ago; today the city remains backlog-free. "We're going to help cities, counties, and states across the country, from coast to coast, to do exactly the same," District Attorney Vance told a roused crowd.[5]

I was very pleased to hear about the fiscal allocation, but I had concerns. What about accountability? How about the rumblings I'd heard about the district attorney's office's earmarked funds being funneled from settlements made with international banks that had violated US sanctions? Would the source of the money pose a problem?

Also, the next presidential election was on my mind. Because federal funding was budgeted only through fiscal year 2016, I worried

4. The New York County District Attorney's Office, "District Attorney Vance Awards $38 Million in Grants to Help 32 Jurisdictions in 20 States Test Backlogged Rape Kits," news release, September 10, 2015, http://manhattanda.org/press-release/district-attorney-vance-awards-38-million-grants-help-32-jurisdictions-20-states-test-.

5. "9.10.15 VP Biden, DA Vance, AG Lynch Announce $79 Million Rape Kit Initiative," YouTube video, 46:34, from a speech given on September 10, 2015, posted by "TheManhattanDA," September 11, 2015, https://www.youtube.com/watch?v=XniKWwuZsUA.

that our presidential candidates might not recognize the importance of continuing the flow of monies to mitigate the backlog. It was troubling that by the spring of that election year, in the melee of debates, caucuses, and seemingly interminable finger-pointing, the issue hadn't been addressed by any presidential candidates, regardless of party affiliation.

At the age of forty-two, for me the media event marked a personal accomplishment on my tumultuous journey from rape to redemption. Two weeks before the press conference, I was asked to be a standby speaker. The day before, I was told that I would *not* be on the roster, but would be an invited guest relegated to the crowd. I didn't really like that idea—I felt that instead of being an active participant, I was going to be more of a prop. I tried to brush it off, but I felt a little sad.

On the way there, Ron, a board member of Natasha's Justice Project, and I missed the train. So Ron agreed to drive us to the event. An unwavering atheist, he cursed furiously at the traffic into New York City as we inched forward. I told Ron that these situations seem to always work out for the best. Before I'd finished the sentence, my cell phone rang. "Could you please speak, after all?" an event organizer asked. I could. After I hung up, Ron and I burst into laughter at the uncanny coincidence.

Now here's the interesting part. I became quite apprehensive as we drew closer to our destination. I couldn't help but feel self-conscious as I thought about what I wanted to say. I second-guessed the outfit I was wearing—a toned-down red crewneck blouse under a conservative gray suit—as well as my hairstyle. My curly hair simply could not be tamed. For every good hair day, I'd have five really awful ones. I also worried that my eyebrows were being unruly and that I just couldn't get my expressive face to be serene and photogenic. In every picture of me speaking I look grumpy or like I'm concentrating too hard, my brow furrowed. Also, I'd gained a little weight. Basically, even though I fight for women and their bodies to be valued every single day, I still hadn't quite figured out how to value my own. How I looked wasn't the important thing, after all—my message was what mattered.

A few months previously, when I'd testified before Congress in mid-June, I'd practiced my speech over and over in front of Scott, my boyfriend of several years. I do a terrible job when speaking from a script, and I'm uncomfortable in one-on-one conversations, especially when it involves bad news. But for some reason, in front of crowds I shine. From elementary school until high school graduation, I won most of the public speaking and debate contests that I entered. Those were my favorite part of academic life. Why then was I jittery this time?

For one, this speech would reach millions, my largest audience so far. With scant time to prepare, I decided to ad-lib it.

"Honey," my mom had sweetly said to me many times, "it's always best when you speak from the soul, from the very depths of your heart." She was right. She'd also told me on numerous occasions, "Always wear clean underwear. You never know what might happen." The irony of that statement wasn't lost on me.

I also remembered how Mom's calling me after each press event became a tradition. After the first conference, she told me how very proud she was to see me on television, standing up for those who couldn't stand up for themselves. "My little Natasha," she said, "how did it feel? How do you feel? What did you do when you got home?"

"Well, Mom, the first thing I did when I got home was clean up dog poo," I told her. We laughed, because no matter how special you feel or how many people are watching you, you still have to come home and clean up the mess the dog left. Now it's a running joke. Immediately after she says hello, Mom asks whether I've cleaned up Piper's poo.

It was nearly time for my turn on the podium when I swallowed water the wrong way and started coughing. Embarrassed when my coughing brought on more coughing, I paused to regroup. I just knew everyone in the crowd could hear my hacking.

Before the press conference had begun, the congresswoman assigned to introduce me had asked how to pronounce my last name. I'd sounded it out phonetically for her: Alex-enko. She wrote it down. Now, in front of dozens of global media representatives, she began her introduction with "My good friend, Alex. Alex Enko." Oops! Her mistake provided comic relief as I took the podium and tried to suppress my lingering coughs.

"Hello," I said, warmly greeting the audience. I always start a speech the same way, with a heartfelt smile and a deep breath. I was grateful as I looked around the crowd, envisioning loved ones who couldn't attend. I kept thinking about Mom. I wanted her there so badly. I suddenly couldn't remember why I had been so nervous.

Something about speaking to a crowd makes me pull from a deep resource that somehow gives me the right words and the right feelings at the right time. It's something akin to a highly focused baseball player at bat, able to tune out all the noise and connect with the ball to hit that home run. The words come from a place that I can only access when I close my eyes and ask myself, *How do I change things for the better?*

After the press conference, Vice President Biden took me aside. He smiled, his blue eyes twinkling as he looked directly into mine. Haltingly he said, "Natasha . . . there are no words." I felt empowered by his response. A very important politician recognized that rape victims mattered! I, a rape survivor, wasn't a freak or a sideshow. In fact, I, as a representative of countless rape victims, *was* the show, the reason that everyone had gathered together. It was time for rape survivors to step out of the shadows and break the silence—it was time for us to speak up.

Of course, violence and suffering are nothing new, nor are resistance and healing and working toward peace. I come from a long line of very strong women who have lived through harrowing circumstances. My maternal grandfather's family, the Mnatzaganians, left Armenia and journeyed to Jerusalem during the Christian Crusades, settling in the fourteenth century A.D. in the Armenian Quarter of Jerusalem and living there for the next nearly seven hundred years.

Meanwhile, the Armenian ancestors of my maternal grandmother had gathered in the part of the Ottoman Empire known today as Turkey. During the early stages of World War I, Russian armies advanced into that region and, citing a looming threat of internal rebellion, the government ordered the demise of all Armenians. In April of 1915, my maternal grandmother, Noyemzar Kchatchadourian, then only four years old, witnessed the slashing of her parents' throats during the Siege of Van.

To make it "more efficient" for the Turks to kill the orphaned children, they dragged them to a large field, where horses were let loose to stampede. After the bloodbath, a distant relative found Noyemzar crouching under a boulder, alive.

It is estimated that during the Armenian Genocide—which Turkey still refuses to acknowledge—an estimated 1.5 million Armenians were slaughtered.[6] By 1917, fewer than 500,000 Armenians remained in Turkey.[7] In his initial presidential bid, in 2008, Barack Obama pledged to officially acknowledge the genocide.[8] Once he was in office, the

---

6. Rouben Paul Adalian, "Armenian Genocide," Armenian National Institute, accessed July 27, 2017, http://www.armenian-genocide.org/genocide.html.

7. Paul Salopek, "A Century Later, Slaughter Still Haunts Turkey and Armenia," *National Geographic*, April 2016.

8. Armenian National Committee of America–National Headquarters, *Barack Obama's Track Record of Armenian Genocide Recognition*, accessed July 6, 2017, https://anca.org/change/docs/Obama_Armenian_Genocide.pdf.

Turkish government threatened to disallow the United States' use of their airspace if he followed through on his word. The plan was abandoned.

My grandmother was taken to an Armenian orphanage in Jerusalem, where she was raised. There, she met and married my grandfather, Joseph Mnatzaganian. My mom, Nevart, was born in the Holy City, along with a brother, David, and two sisters, Jean and Marianna. In the winter, the family lived in Jericho, by the West Bank near the Jordan River, where they managed several farms and owned a barbershop. Summers were spent in the Armenian Quarter in Jerusalem, located in the walled Old City, until another political conflict—the Six-Day War—turned their world upside down.

During the short but deadly battle, also known as the June War or the 1967 Arab-Israeli War, Mom and her parents were forced to flee Jericho, all the while dodging bullets and bodies on their passage to Jerusalem. While fleeing, a cousin was hit in the head by shrapnel. He still bears a deep scar.

My mother—like her mother before her—was a witness to unspeakable horror. For the sake of Mom's safety and out of a desire for her to have a better life, my maternal grandmother, whom I would know as "Neh-Neh," encouraged her to emigrate to America. Mom earned a scholarship to Messiah College, a Mennonite school in Pennsylvania, and initially planned to study pharmacology. Because English wasn't her second or even third language, Mom earned a home economics degree instead. In college, she met and married my dad, Victor Alexenko, who was earning a degree in social work.

In 1970, Mom's family scattered to the far reaches of the globe. David, Marianna, and Neh-Neh moved to Canada; Jean and her family relocated to Australia. It was difficult for Mom's close-knit relatives to live nearly 9,000 miles apart, but war and necessity brought about the separation, and they were glad simply to be alive.

My father's side of the family was also lucky to have survived their own ordeal in Europe. My paternal grandfather, Symon (pronounced "SEE-moan") Kakoshin, was a physicist, whom the government eventually sent to freeze in Siberia. When World War II started, my paternal grandmother, Vera Kakoshin, whom I would know as "Babushka," fled Russia to Poland with my father, then a small boy. The story of what happened next is somewhat hazy. Mom and I have done our best to piece together the mystery of those years, but Babushka was quite secretive, and she never really told us what happened. We definitely know that the two of them somehow landed in a concentration camp, but we don't know exactly where or why. We speculate that because my grandmother spoke German fluently, she may have survived by helping with Russian-German translation. Plus, she received reparation checks from Germany, which means that she was a victim of some kind, and definitely not a collaborator.

Convinced her husband was dead and buried under the Siberian tundra, Babushka became involved with Anatoli "Tony" Alexenko at the German concentration camp. Together they planned to escape to America, where they would marry, find work, and provide their son with a proper education. Somehow they made it to New York—again, the details are hazy—and found jobs on a factory assembly line until they'd saved enough money to buy a motel and two gas stations. No matter her income or assets, Babushka lived like a beggar, and later in her life she constantly told us how poor they'd been. She also became something of a hoarder, which I discovered when I moved into the family home in Islip, New York, in 2004. While giving the house a thorough cleaning, I found hundreds of thousands of dollars stuffed under mattresses. By then Babushka had developed Alzheimer's disease, and this newfound money paid for her retirement in a nursing home in Canada. It was quite expensive, at $6,000 a month minimum, but she was kept clean and fed, and she had her hair done once a week. In an odd way, she was finally able to enjoy the money she'd squirreled away for all those years.

I'm amazed by how much adversity my family had to overcome for me to be here. I was born on a Wednesday in 1973 at Good Samaritan Hospital on Long Island, New York, bringing with me "a good dose of joy," according to Mom. It was February, and the weather was bitterly cold, with the lowest temperatures hovering around zero degrees Fahrenheit. In a short succession of blasts, snow had stacked to over a foot high. Even though March 10 was her due date, Mom worried the icy weather wouldn't clear before she went into labor.

Unfortunately, another storm was raging inside their home in Islip. The morning before my birth, my drug-addicted father pushed Mom down the stairs. Bruised but without broken bones, Mom carried on with her daily chores. Because she had never seen illegal drugs or narcotics, she didn't understand why Dad was acting so strangely, and she stayed in denial about his very serious problem. Labor pains came on strong while Mom was feeding the chickens in our big backyard coop a few hours later. Mom told Babushka, who had dropped by the house, that she was going into labor. Babushka accused Mom of being dramatic, turned on her heel, and went back to the house she shared with Tony at one of their motel properties. Dad was nowhere to be found.

Before the night's end, Tony drove Mom to the hospital, and I came along at 4:00 a.m. on February 28. Dad was wired out of his mind when he showed up a few hours later to see me for the first time. A nurse who spoke Armenian noticed his erratic behavior and the bruises on Mom's body and told her in their native tongue, "Your husband isn't right. I'm going to say that you're not ready to go home so you can stay here in safety for a few days."

While in the hospital, Mom called Neh-Neh to ask her to help care for me. Then she planned our escape from Dad.

In Jerusalem, Mom had worked for the United Nations, where she'd met a group of Mennonite missionaries. Remembering that they lived in Pennsylvania, Mom called them for help; they immediately came to rescue us. Until we moved to Canada a few months later, we stayed with our Mennonite friends. Even though we attended Mennonite services, Mom went to a Mennonite college, and the Mennonites were very dear to us and a constant fixture in my early years, she continued practicing her Armenian Orthodox faith.

After we crossed the Canadian border in 1975, we lived in the restaurant of a motel that was closed for the season, thanks to the Mennonites who'd found us this temporary home until Mom could secure a job and a green card. As a toddler, I was very curious and precocious. I remember discovering bathrooms for men *and* women in our "house" and being fascinated by the men's restroom. I imagined all the secrets it might contain.

After Uncle David sponsored Mom's citizenship, our lives began anew. St. Catharines in Ontario had a very large Armenian community, which embraced us with open arms. Soon, Mom found work as a dietician for an organization that was like the Canadian equivalent of an American juvenile detention center. She worked mostly with children under the age of sixteen; many had experienced some kind of trauma themselves.

Once settled, Mom befriended Vaughn and Lucy Osgan, whose four-year-old son, Vaughn Jr., became my lifelong best friend. Because both of us were only children, and I was a year younger, he and I grew up as close as siblings. We even fought like brother and sister; he threatened to take away my stuffed animals if I didn't behave myself! We also got into trouble together, even destroying invaluable antique furniture as a result of our antics. No treasured piece was safe from us. We spent every holiday together with the Osgans as one family: Vaughn Sr. was my male role model, and my mom was thrilled that I had a father figure in my life. He was one of the first people to get me into reading, giving me books by some of the greats, like Alfred Lord Tennyson, Mary Shelley, Lord Byron, Percy Shelley, Henry Miller, William S. Burroughs, and Shakespeare. He even had a beautiful print of "The Lady of Shalott" framed for me. We'd talk at length about these books—to me he was the smartest man in the world, so literary and charming. I read *Hamlet*, and during a discussion about it he said to me, "Don't be an Ophelia." Decades later, I would remember that conversation after having to face some hard truths about Vaughn Sr.'s character.

While Mom worked, Neh-Neh raised me. She was the gentlest woman I've ever known. Because Neh-Neh didn't speak English, I only spoke Armenian until I was five years old. Then Neh-Neh had a stroke. A bad one. The day she returned home from the rehabilitation center, I was a happy little girl, assuming that I'd immediately continue my ritual of waking at dawn and jumping into Neh-Neh's bed. The first morning back, Mom stopped me. Neh-Neh was snoring loudly, and Mom wanted her to continue resting. My persistent begging paid off and Mom finally relented. But when I hopped on Neh-Neh's bed, she didn't budge. I called out her name. Nothing. I moved closer and noticed her skin was blue. "Mom," I said as I raced into her room, "Neh-Neh won't wake up!"

A few moments later, I heard Mom shriek and then pound her fists against the wall, crying out Neh-Neh's name. Seeing Mom's tears made me cry, even though I was too young to fully comprehend what had occurred. The family physician, Dr. Lorenzen, who once served as the local coroner, made a house call to confirm Neh-Neh's passing. I don't recall much after that. I was sent to stay with a local Mennonite family, the Days, so Mom could take care of business. She rented a new apartment, moved everything into it, collected me, and, once again, our lives started over.

Forty days after Neh-Neh's death, Uncle David had a fatal heart attack. He was only forty-one, and Mom took his passing hard. I was again sent to the Days' house for a while.

I have no recollection of Dad during this time, but I remember noticing his absence. Later I wondered how a father could have *not* rushed to his daughter's side when her mother was going through such pain. And where was Babushka? Of course, Mom was fiercely independent. I don't know if she even asked for help.

One evening when I was nine years old, I was stepping out of the shower when I heard Mom crying. I had only seen her cry twice: when Neh-Neh died, and then when Uncle David died.

"What's wrong?" I asked. "Did my dad die?" Mom gave me an incredulous look. "How did you know?" she said.

Honestly, I'm not sure how I knew. I'd been told that he was "sick" and that that was the reason I only saw him occasionally. I later found out that Dad had been working as a drug counselor at the time. He'd relapsed and overdosed.

I don't recall crying or feeling overly sad about Dad's death. I remember not saying "I love you" when he and I had spoken on the phone for what would turn out to be the last time. That fact still haunts me. To this day, I never hang up with a loved one without saying it. If Mom hangs up before I get a chance to tell her, I always call back and say, "I love you."

Shortly before Dad's death, my hamster died. I was devastated by the loss of my tiny pet. I was a mess! *Why,* I wondered, *didn't I have the same reaction to the death of the man who gave me life?* I felt guilty that I'd hardly shed a tear for Dad but had cried myself to sleep over little Hammy. Even now, when anything tragic happens to me, it's as if all the pain of those past misfortunes returns in full force, even the grief over my hamster. The pain washes over me and the mourning begins all over again.

I wish I could say my elementary school experience was a good one, but it wasn't, at least not at first. Because Mom was full-blooded Armenian and I have a very Russian name, I was bullied relentlessly. Mom's status as a single mother in a family-oriented community where the vast majority of the population worked at the local General Motors assembly plant didn't help much. My classmates would ask, "Why are you different?" in various ways, but it came down to the same bottom line: I *was* different, and no one let me forget it, especially during the Cold War in the mid-1980s. I remember being taught in the fourth grade that Russians were bad people. If Russians were bad, what did that say about me?

Still, somehow, I won the role of sidekick to Dori Anderson, the most popular girl in our class. A full-blooded Canadian, Dori was petite, with long curly blonde hair, and she was always dressed to the nines. Dori's father sold luxury cars and always drove a Porsche, Mercedes-Benz, or the like. They had the biggest house and the only swimming pool in our neighborhood, and her epic birthday parties were talked about all year long. Meanwhile, I'd grown faster than my schoolmates, becoming the tallest in my class, and my mom and I didn't exactly have the funds for nice clothes or fancy cars. Dori and I made quite a pair.

Together we spent many afternoons playing in the woods, coming up with all kinds of stories underneath the huge willow trees. We made up our own world, very much like Narnia of The Chronicles of Narnia series by C. S. Lewis. Our alternative universe held secret passageways and special characters. That is, until the parents of some other kids found out and got upset, apparently because we'd crossed a religious line. Two teachers as well as the principal took us aside and told us to stop playing pretend, that it was anti-Christian. What! It didn't make sense to me; we weren't doing anything wrong.

Still, that was the end of our friendship.

After that, I spent more time alone, my nose in a book, usually one given to me by Vaughn Sr. As I grew older, the fantasy world I'd created with Dori faded from my mind. High school opened my eyes to new worlds that, until then, had been turning outside of my awareness, as well as other fantasies to pay attention to.

I met Trevor Ballin at the age of fourteen. We were instantly attached at the hip. We liked the same music, art, and literature, and we spent most of our time together daydreaming about moving to New York City. Trevor wanted to be a fashion designer; I flirted with the idea of studying film or journalism.

Happily absorbed in the pastime of inventing a future, I was more than a little put out when Mom told me we were going on an adventure in the summer of my fifteenth year. We'd be staying with Aunt Jean in Sydney, Australia, she said. I didn't want to go. Leave my friends? No way. Leave my books? As if.

Australia's east coast is absolutely beautiful. Sydney is home to one of the world's largest natural harbors, and majestic mountains sprawl to the west. Being with my cousins Taleen and Anthony and my amazing aunt Jean are moments I will cherish forever. You know those random funny occurrences that have you laughing so hard you can barely breathe? We had more of those than I can count. I felt such a kinship with my Australian relatives. Although I loved my Canadian family members, I felt as though my cousins from Down Under were cut from the same cloth as I was. Of course, by the time Australia's winter—Canada's summer—came to a close, I didn't want to leave. I begged Mom to let me stay. She might have thought about it briefly, but sadly we didn't miss our flight home.

I was glad to get home. I'd missed Vaughn Jr. and his family. Around that time, I met another like-minded friend, Kyle Bingley. A few years older than me, Kyle was openly gay. Trevor and Kyle had similar interests, so I was excited to introduce them to each other. I was a bit surprised when Kyle took me aside and asked, "Is Trevor gay?" A light bulb went on! I'd never thought about Trevor's sexuality.

Together the three of us ventured to Gustos, the only gay bar in St. Catharines. Turned out, Gusto's was a safe space for us to just be ourselves. We felt accepted, protected, part of a special community that didn't judge us. Folks even thought my Russian background was interesting, not threatening!

We didn't need alcohol to have a good time. We danced freely, intoxicated by our youth. That night, Trevor came out to me, and thus began our regular trips to Gusto's. Mom even joined us for pride parades. She and I became honorary members of the gay community. It was a happy, free time.

Then, in 1992, during my senior year, Kristen French, a fifteen-year-old schoolmate, was abducted in front a church across from the apartment building where Mom and I lived. Paul Bernardo, also known as the "Scarborough Rapist" and "Schoolgirl Killer," and Karla Homolka had formed the psychopathic husband-and-wife team later to be known as the "Ken and Barbie Killers." For three days they filmed themselves torturing this much-loved classmate, and later her body was discovered in a ditch. The police used our balcony to survey the area.

I can't convey the horror of this crime or say enough to honor Kristen's memory. She was, like so many girls on the verge of adulthood, energetic and beautiful and full of potential. She had a life ahead of her, and it was stolen from her. Her murder was a terrible tragedy, one that was—and is and will forever be—etched into my memory, but at that time I was young and not easily deterred. Even though I now know the next awful chapter of my life story, I admire the fearlessness that I had at the time. If I could, would I tell the younger version of myself to not go out into the world, to stay safe? Obviously nowhere on earth, even the relatively small city of St. Catharines, was immune to tragedy. And, anyway, what would this world be like if women didn't pursue their dreams, regardless of the danger?

Moving to New York City after graduation seemed like a good way to get a fresh start. I was undaunted when my new roommate told me, "In New York City, there's not enough room to hold someone captive for three days. Here you just get killed!"

I was confident. Nothing bad would happen to me.

2.

The Seventh Floor

*"It's not that I don't trust you; it's just that
I don't trust everyone else."*
—Mom

When I was a teenager, Babushka was a juror in a New York County trial for a man accused of rape. My Russian grandmother explained, in her broken English, "Natasha, rape . . . not possible. *Think!* If you try to thread a needle and the needle is constantly always moving, it cannot be done. No good." Unfortunately, Babushka was not alone in this belief, nor did she make up this analogy—many credit nineteenth-century gynecologist Lawson Tait for saying, "You cannot thread a moving needle." Years later, these words tormented me as I was being violated.

Hours before the rape, I was on the clock as a veterinary technician at the Riverside Animal Hospital on West 108th Street. It was one of several jobs that I worked to make ends meet between classes at the

New York Institute of Technology, where I was studying filmmaking. I also walked dogs in my spare time. I'd purposely sought work involving animals to see if veterinary medicine might be a fit for me, especially after hearing from so many "well-meaning" people that women don't make films.

I'd moved to New York City fifty-one weeks earlier and found an apartment on the Upper West Side to share with Jim and Cecilia Crisp, a couple I'd met through the want ads. They needed to lease a large room in their huge prewar apartment to offset the area's high rent. Adorably, they'd signed their ad "Cecilia, Jimmy, and dog Mickey." I loved them immediately. Plus, I'd always wanted a dog, and they said I could get one. So I brought home Savannah, a pit bull and gentle giant.

Living in the city was like being in Narnia, almost like being back in that magical fantasy world I'd imagined as a kid. We didn't have such distinct seasons up in Ontario; in New York, for the first time I watched each season go by, expressed in all its glory. Everything was so vibrant and bigger than life—the changing colors of the leaves in the fall, the way the snow blanketed the city in winter. Spring's scent was delicious and fresh, and summer was the greenest of greens.

I loved the location—in Manhattan between Central Park and the Hudson River. The energy of the city was contagious. We didn't have to wait until a Saturday night at Gusto's to have a good time. Bars pulsing with music and like-minded people were around every corner. Nearly every city block was self-sufficient, and even we rookie New Yorkers only needed to go past the invisible demarcation line for school, work, or entertainment.

The borough, the building, and the Crisps had met with Mom's approval. Because rent was slightly cheaper than that at neighboring high-rises, we didn't have a doorman. Instead, we had a two-step entry from the street. Two sets of locked double-glass doors provided some measure of safety. Mom was satisfied that that would be enough.

My apartment building was adjacent to Riverside Park, which boasts Manhattan's most spectacular view of the Hudson, which in my humble opinion is more magical than Central Park. Lush plantings border serpentine paths, and I often took Savannah to the park's fenced-in dog run. At night, streetlights glowed, lighting up the majestic oaks, their leaves sparkling as though there were gems hidden within. The four-mile boulevard was speckled with magnolia trees, more sprawling oaks, and cherry blossoms.

Another draw to Riverside Park was the statues of many important historical figures with a connection to the Big Apple. Grant's Tomb is there, along with an Eleanor Roosevelt monument. Not far away is a rocky outcropping frequented by Edgar Allan Poe, whose macabre tales had kept me mesmerized on many a long Canadian night. A statue of Joan of Arc is displayed prominently, and I'd often stop to read her story, even though I'd quickly learned it by heart. Nicknamed the "Maid of Orléans," the Roman Catholic saint was a heroine of France during the Hundred Years' War. She reported seeing visions of the archangel Michael, Saint Margaret, and Saint Catherine, visions that urged her to support Charles VII and recover France from English domination. What a bold woman! I wanted to be like her.

On that dreadful night, I locked up the veterinarian's office around 9:30 p.m. I raced to meet my girlfriend Amy at the West End Bar on the corner of 113th Street and Broadway. As my heels clicked in a rhythmic pace on the sidewalk, I peeled off the cardigan I'd worn in the clinic where the air conditioning was constantly on full blast and tried to adjust to the late-summer heat and humidity outside.

While nursing one-dollar drafts, Amy and I chatted about the usual stuff—school, friends, and boys. Around eleven o'clock, Amy and I headed to her apartment at West 112th Street between Broadway and Amsterdam. Knowing I had class the next morning, followed by work at the animal hospital until closing time, I left before midnight. The taxi stopped at the corner of Broadway and West 95th Street, and I headed west to my apartment building while digging in my purse for keys.

Normally, I would've paid more attention to my surroundings, just as Mom had preached before I left Canada. But that night my sights were set on the park. I was thinking about the next day, about making a beeline home from school so that I could take Savannah along its serpentine walkway to the doggy playground. I was so engrossed in my thoughts that, for all I know, the stranger who would do me harm had been following me the entire time.

Let's pause here for a second. Like I've said, every survivor has a choice about how they want to talk, or not talk, about their rape. For me, secrecy and shame around my experience have caused me a lot of suffering, and I've come to a point where talking openly and even explicitly is part of my healing process. Writing this book is part of that process, as is trying to help other survivors. So I am going to describe what happened to me in detail. If that is a trigger for you, please skip ahead to chapter three.

I fished out the key to the first entrance, unlocked the door, and walked into the vestibule. I didn't notice a presence behind me until I felt an object pressed against my back. Then I felt hot, stale breath on the nape of my neck.

"Listen to me," the stranger said harshly, his voice low. "If you don't do everything I say, I'll blow your goddamn brains out."

Fear nearly buckled my knees and I faltered. I had trouble getting past the second set of doors. While I fumbled with the key, he gave me an incentive.

"Look at this gun," he sneered, shoving a 9mm handgun under my nose. "See these gold bullets? See this slide? All I have to do is . . ."

His voice trailed off. He didn't need to finish the sentence. I got it. I unlocked the second door.

In the lobby, I got my first good look at my assailant. He was black, about six feet tall, with short dreadlocks framing an oval face that showed a hint of the mustache he was trying to grow. He was surprisingly clean cut and lean, around 175 pounds, with a black backpack slung over one shoulder. He spoke with a distinctive New York accent.

"What floor do you live on?" he asked gruffly. "Do you live alone? How many roommates do you have?"

I frantically scrambled to come up with something off-putting to his series of questions. I told him I had two roommates and two dogs. He shoved me toward the elevator and asked if I knew how to get to the roof. "No," I lied, while looking around for help. It was a little after midnight. *Where is everybody?* I thought. A surge of panic took over and my eyes brimmed with tears. "Are you going to hurt me?" I asked in a faltering voice. Any moment now, I hoped, a neighbor would step out of his or her door and rescue me. Then I'd go up to my apartment, count my lucky stars, get a good night's sleep, and share the story with my roommates in the morning.

That scenario didn't play out.

"I'm just trying to hide from the cops, and I need a place to stay," the stranger said.

Phew! I thought. *OK, then. Maybe he really does just want a place to lay low for a little while. Now that we're inside, he'll let me go. If not, maybe I can get the attention of the doorman across the street.* But apparently Gene Paranuk didn't see anything. Later, when questioned by the police, the veteran doorman reported that he'd clocked in at midnight at the high-rise apartment building directly across the street and noticed no unusual activity. He refused to provide his home address or phone number.

We kept going, and I started sobbing. Tears streamed down my cheeks. The man angrily jabbed a finger at the elevator panel, hitting the button to the highest floor, the seventh. Normally, the unmanned elevator moves at a snail's pace, irritatingly slow and with constipated stops between floors. Unlike typical elevators, this one didn't roost on the lobby floor when not in use. *This* time, however, with a quickness I'd never seen, the elevator doors parted. My stomach sank when I saw it was empty. As we were ascending, he shoved me against the back wall of the platform, then spun me around so he was positioned behind me. When I whimpered, a dig in my back with the muzzle of the gun shut me up again. The elevator may as well have been a cage.

On the painstakingly slow crawl to the top floor, I kept my head down, staring at his black shoes. *Maybe, just maybe, someone is waiting for the elevator on one of these floors. It'll open, and I'll be spared.* But there were no stops. Instead, the doors opened on the seventh floor, and he shoved me up a set of steps, stopping abruptly on a small landing leading to the roof. He scrutinized the special door lock, wired with an alarm device. Fearful of setting off a siren, he pushed me around the landing to the top of the stairwell. *Maybe a neighbor will take the stairs any minute,* I thought hopefully.

My neighbors were nowhere to be seen or heard. In the apartment closest to the elevator bank, unit 71, John and Aliza Glustram heard nothing. Ramsey Ghurzeddine in unit 72 had walked his dog around midnight, returned home, and led his pet to a room farthest from the hallway. If he'd been nearer, the dog would've alerted Ramsey or his roommate, Kevin Hill, to unusual goings-on in the hallway. Unit 73 was empty. Michale Postel in unit 74 was home all evening, but oblivious to the outside world. If she'd heard anything, she'd simply turned up the volume on her TV. Theresa Earenfight in unit 75 didn't arrive home until the predawn hours. Another neighbor was blissfully asleep, and yet another spoke Spanish only. Without a translator, he was no help.

The dank, dark stairwell was concrete and metal and reeking of alcohol and urine, amplified by the summer's humidity. I'd avoided this creepy place in the nighttime. Now I was nauseous. The stranger ordered me to remove my scrub shirt, and he wasn't deterred when I threw up. Instead, he shoved the gun closer to my face. When he told me to remove my bra, shorts, and underwear, swells of panic filled my throat. I could hardly catch my breath.

"Do as I say and you'll be OK," he repeated as he grabbed my cash, subway tokens, and gold cross necklace. I felt a sharp pang when he stole the cross—my father had given it to Mom shortly after I was born; it was the only thing of his I carried with me.

For a fleeting moment, I thought that's all the stranger wanted—cash and items to pawn—so he could buy alcohol or drugs or whatever his habit required. *Maybe he had me undress so I wouldn't run after him,* I thought, still in denial about the probable outcome of this awful situation. I'd always been a very modest person. I didn't even like wearing a bathing suit at the public pool. Standing there naked, I was mortified. *Now he'll leave,* I hoped. Instead, he unzipped his green jeans and pulled out his penis. Disgust washed over me. *This isn't happening!* Funny how the mind operates—amidst the fear and revulsion, I couldn't help but notice the odd color of his jeans. And, since I didn't know his name, to me he became Mr. Green Jeans.

Mr. Green Jeans ordered me to suck it and told me that if I bit it, he'd blow my brains out. My heart sank. My head ached. My mind raced. *How can I get away?* I asked myself, then tried to reassure myself when I couldn't come up with an answer. *OK, I can do this. Then he'll let me go.* I reluctantly took his penis in my trembling hand, closed my eyes, and put my mouth over it. I gagged at the vile taste. Once aroused, he yanked me up, pushed me around, and shoved my body against the cold, rusty banister. We already had the next part down pat: I sobbed; he told me to shut up. Even though he spoke only in whispers, his words silenced my pleas.

While I was being raped, I stared down the winding staircase to the floors below. The black and white tiles on each floor created an optical illusion that reminded me of Alice in Wonderland peering down the seemingly endless rabbit hole. I didn't have a fear of heights until that moment. The sight made me dizzy. I closed my eyes and imagined being at Birdland, a dark and intimate smoke-filled jazz bar that I loved. Even though I was underage, the waitstaff often let me hang around for hours. I loved it when the musicians improvised; they seemed to have so much fun. I pictured the jazzman on the saxophone, suspended in wisps of smoke. It helped me remain steady.

At times during the forty-five-minute assault, I felt a comforting sensation, like a bright light cascading from the ceiling and enveloping me. I'm not sure if it was real or imagined, but it was so vivid. I felt a peace wash over me, a gift from a power much greater than me or this angry stranger. Every now and then a burst of pain would snap me back to reality. Mr. Green Jeans alternated between telling me "Relax, shhh" and "I'm going to fucking blow your goddamn brains out!" My thoughts fluctuated from *OK, just be calm,* to panic and a feeling of abandonment. When I'd cry, he'd get rougher. Then I'd bite my tongue to hold back my tears, until another burst of pain caused me to start crying again. This was the cycle that played out over and over.

He abruptly stepped back and told me to put on my clothes. Because Mr. Green Jeans didn't make a sound that indicated so, I wasn't sure he'd ejaculated. The gun remained firmly pointed at my temple. I hesitated before leaning over to gather my scattered clothing, my only layer of protection. *Maybe it's a trick,* I thought, feeling even more exposed. And then I realized, *I've seen his face. I can identify him. Why wouldn't he just kill me?* I played out the scenario in my mind. Mom would be absolutely devastated, perhaps beyond recovery. I certainly didn't want to leave this world in such a way. Another statistic. A life not fully lived.

I was relieved when he ran off down the stairs. But he paused midway to deliver the threat: "Don't come after me or I'll kill you!"

I grabbed my clothes and ran to my apartment as fast as my wobbly legs would allow. I was so disoriented; my feet got tangled and I stumbled several times, twice falling into the wall. But I kept running down those hideous stairs.

I remember banging on my apartment door and being relieved when it swung open right away. Later, Jimmy told me that he couldn't shake a recurring nightmare about my bloodcurdling scream as I collapsed inside in a heap, wailing and whimpering and speaking incoherent gibberish. My roommates were awake because Savannah had been fretting inconsolably for nearly an hour. Usually quiet, she'd been agitated the whole time I was being assaulted. That knowledge still breaks my heart. Savannah *knew* something bad was happening to me. For the rest of her life, she was my shadow. She was the noblest animal I'd ever known.

Blaring sirens and blinding lights are the last details I remember about the ordeal.

I don't remember the ambulance ride, or my arrival at the hospital. But I do remember the emergency waiting room, where I sat for what felt like hours. Cilia took a break from her pacing to ask a nurse if I could call my mother. In the nurse's station I dialed my mother's number—*my* number just a short year before. She answered quickly with a panicked "Hello?" I could tell she knew something was wrong; calls in the middle of the night rarely bring good news.

I just couldn't tell her. The words would not leave my lips. I handed the phone to Cilia and I heard her say it.

"Natasha was raped at gunpoint and we are in the hospital."

My legs gave out from under me. Suddenly I felt as though I was breathing underwater. The nurses scrambled around me to make certain I was all right. I wasn't. Hearing Cilia utter those words out loud made everything *real*. All at once I recognized what had just occurred, how much worse things could have gone, and that things would never be the same again.

The scene I was making was enough to move me from the general waiting area to a room of my own where it was about to become clear to me—my body was a crime scene.

A rape kit exam is not an easy procedure to undergo. Collecting evidence in this manner is basically like a very invasive gynecological exam. In addition to being poked and prodded, you are asked intimate questions regarding the assault. As you can imagine, this is particularly difficult when you have just gone through such a traumatic event.

The Sexual Assault Nurse Examiner (SANE) could not have been kinder. In my opinion, the men and women who perform these exams are nothing short of heroic. From the onset, I was treated with kindness and respect, and I attribute much of my healing to those first responders. I didn't feel coddled or pitied. I felt that a gentle caregiver was inviting me to be a part of the crime-solving team that would eventually find the man who raped me and lock him away forever. In my case, the SANE assigned to me set the tone for how things would continue going forward.

I have since had the great honor of meeting SANE and SART (Sexual Assault Response Team) professionals. In Long Island, New York, where I currently reside, we are fortunate enough to have a SANE Center at Stony Brook University Hospital. These hospitals can say they have a SANE Center when they offer comprehensive medical care for sexual assault victims. Forensic examinations are conducted in a private setting, where an interdisciplinary team involving a hospital-based Sexual Assault Forensic Examiner (SAFE) program, a rape crisis center, law enforcement, the prosecutor's office, and other appropriate service agencies are available to meet the needs of the survivor as well as improve the overall community response to sexual assault. Stony Brook University Hospital even has a shower! Unfortunately, such luxuries are still the exception and not the rule across the country.

After the rape kit exam, the detectives arrived. They asked me to describe the man who raped me. Every time I tried to recall his face, it morphed, and I'm certain his description changed each time I was asked for it. I also had to describe the rape itself. I had to talk about my body—the crime scene—as though it were a park or something of that nature in which I'd witnessed a crime. As though it hadn't happened to me, as though I just *saw* it happen. Identifying exactly what I saw and in what order was a surreal experience, my first in terms of disconnecting from what had occurred. My thoughts were jumbled, and I couldn't keep things straight. Did it occur here, or did it occur there? Did this happen first, or did that happen before? My mind started playing tricks on me, and I began doubting my own account of the ordeal. In an act of self-preservation, my brain had started to go off-line. It was just too much to handle. Still, despite my hazy memory, I was treated with a great deal of patience and respect.

This is usually where survivors' narratives diverge. The way I was cared for was unique, especially for 1993. Unfortunately, often the crime and the victim are not taken seriously, even more so when the complaining witness in a sexual assault contradicts their own statements. Sometimes victims are simply dismissed as liars. People addicted to drugs or alcohol, sex workers, people who are homeless, wards of the state, and people with mental illnesses are more likely to face this kind of treatment. People of color, too. I have heard police say they didn't believe someone because she wasn't crying, or she wasn't crying enough, or she was crying too much. I have seen reports where the survivor was dismissed as an unreliable witness because she didn't fit the perceived notions of how a victim *should* act. This isn't to say police have bad intentions—quite the contrary. It comes down to training: most police officers I've met who've been through rape crisis training say it changed their whole outlook on sexual assault, trauma, and memory and prepared them to better manage the situation and care for the victim.

After the exam and intense questioning session, I was given antibiotics and antivirals as a first line of defense against STDs. I was told I would need to be tested for HIV at six-month intervals for ten years. And since I wasn't on any sort of birth control, I'd need to keep an eye on my next period to make certain I hadn't become pregnant. I hadn't thought of that possibility, and I wept.

When I was asked if there was anything I needed, a new emotion flooded over me: anger. This wasn't the run-of-the-mill kind—this was like a primal rage. All the fight I'd held back, trumped by my fear of being killed, now erupted, at least internally. Even after all I'd been through, I was still aware of my surroundings and, subconsciously, what was expected of me. I imagine someone else—a man, perhaps—would yell or cuss or smash a wall or scream. I wanted to hit the monster who'd raped me, but of course he wasn't there. Instead, I paced while trying to swallow the bile rising in my throat. *How could he have done this to me?* I thought over and over again. *How could he have done this to me how could he have done this to me how could he have done this to me?* I felt as though I had been possessed by a demon—but I had no outlet to express the anger that was like a volcano erupting inside me, and I probably wouldn't have known how even if I believed I could. It hurt so much. So I did the only thing I, a former Catholic schoolgirl, could: I asked for a priest.

The priest they brought around wasn't much older than me. He had these huge round glasses, the lenses so thick that his eyes looked like pebbles behind them. They darted back and forth as I explained this anger welling up inside me.

"I need help," I said. "I need God or something to take it away. Please, help me."

"I—I—I don't—I don't know what to say," he stuttered, clearly terrified. "I'm only here at the hospital to give last rites."

"Please, pray with me," I said. "It will give me strength."

His posture changed at that suggestion. Once again empowered to tend to an injured member of his flock, he closed his eyes. Together we prayed for God to forgive whoever raped me.

Now I realize how backward that was. We didn't pray for *me*—not for my healing or for God to give me strength or for God to protect me. Instead we prayed for forgiveness for this monster who didn't give a shit about me, my body, my spirit, my life. Do you think he thought for one second about me afterward? Do you think he felt even one pang of guilt? I doubt it.

Yet our prayers did bring me relief, because forgiveness has always been my go-to coping mechanism. It's much more comfortable for me to forgive those who hurt me than stand up for myself or express my anger or fight back. I was well trained to be the demure young woman I was supposed to be. It is an impulse I continue to struggle with to this day.

After the priest left, I changed into the clothing that my roommates had brought for me. Everything I'd been wearing that night was now part of the crime scene, evidence tucked away in plastic bags. SANE will often provide new clothing for survivors who have undergone a rape kit exam. Hospitals without SANE are not always so accommodating; I have heard horror stories from survivors who had to ride the bus home from the hospital in nothing but a paper gown.

Years into the future, my underwear would make its grand debut in the HBO documentary *Sex Crimes Unit*. I am grateful that the viewers saw a modest pair of underwear, neither granny nor thong. The first time my mother saw it on film, she leaned over and whispered to me:

"That's a nice pair of underwear. Do you think they would give them back to you?"

Returning to the apartment was strange. There were still police everywhere. Our normally quiet building, where no one really socialized, was full of groups of tenants whispering to one another in the hallways. I tried to shrug off the uneasy feeling that my life would never be the same again. I just wanted to go back to my apartment and listen to Nina Simone, but I recognized her music would forever sound different to me.

Anyone will tell you that New Yorkers stick together like no other people in the world. The next few days, as I tried to pull my life together, I was greeted with incredible compassion and warmth. I was invited for drinks, dinners, and movie nights by the other tenants. People brought me cookies, cakes, and flowers. The couple across the street whose dog I walked brought me a cross to replace the one my rapist had stolen—a gesture that is forever imprinted upon my heart. Such kindness I cannot find the words to describe.

Jane was one tenant I will never forget. We had passed one another in the past without making eye contact. I knew that she lived in one of the basement apartments, and that she had a sense of style I admired. One day, soon after the rape, she approached me and invited me to her place for coffee.

Her apartment was filled with books and antiques. It felt comfortable and lived in, a clear reflection of its owner. With steaming mugs in hand we sat down on the floor, and she shared a story from her past, a story similar to mine. I had met my first fellow survivor.

Jane didn't claim to have the answers, or a miracle cure for the fear and panic. She did have a cross, though, that someone had given to her after her assault. She placed it in my hand and gently closed my fingers around it. Her hands felt tiny and cold. I promised I would keep it safe until the time came when I no longer needed it. Like she had done, at that time I would pass it along to someone who needed it more than I did.

Two years later, I gave that cross to my very first therapist, after she'd announced that she'd be leaving her practice because she'd been diagnosed with stomach cancer. It felt like it was meant to be. Several years later, I received a postcard from her, on which she wrote that she, too, had passed the cross along, and that she was currently in remission. I often think about that cross, wondering if it is still going from survivor to survivor, a small token of comfort during whatever trial they're going through.

I really tried my best to return to "normal," and I thought I was doing a pretty good job of fooling everyone. Truthfully, I felt like I was hanging off a cliff, my fingers slipping, and solid ground miles below. Keeping up the pretense was exhausting. The toll it was taking must have been more obvious than I thought, because while I was telling my mother everything was fine, my roommates were telling her otherwise.

A week after my rape and one year to the day I'd moved into my apartment at 336 West 95th Street, my mother showed up in a rental van. Savannah and I were moving back to Canada.

3.

MASK OF NORMALCY

"I don't care how everyone else is doing;
I care about how you're doing."
—Mom

Today I know that moving back to Canada likely saved my life. At twenty, I felt as though my dreams were over, that the possibilities of a future had been ripped from my grasp. I didn't want people to know what had happened to me. And after a high school friend accused me of lying about being raped as an excuse to come home, I decided to hide my secret deep inside. Trevor, Kyle, and Vaughn Jr. were the few friends to whom I told the truth.

My high school sweetheart, Matt, and I reunited to disastrous results. We'd met in grade thirteen, which was the final year of secondary school in Ontario at the time. He was good-looking and outgoing, and I'd hardly been able to believe that he liked me back. Our high school romance was the usual kind—intense, a little bit messy, passionate. His mom never liked me, for whatever reason, but his dad, who worked for the fire department, was one of those people who loves and is loved by all.

Matt and I had decided to stay together after I'd revealed my plans of moving to New York City, and in the beginning of our separation, he would come to the city to visit me every other week. It was a great way to continue my ties to home. He'd tell me all the gossip about our high school friends, and I'd show him all the cool places I was discovering in Manhattan.

Then his father died suddenly while shoveling snow from a neighbor's driveway. Just like that, he dropped dead. After that my boyfriend became someone I didn't recognize. That carefree, happy-go-lucky goofball disappeared, replaced by an angry person with a big chip on his shoulder. It was the craziest thing—and it speaks to trauma and how it affects those who experience it.

When I told Matt what had happened to me, he said, "My father dies and then my girlfriend gets raped? What is wrong with the world?" I can't imagine it was easy for him to have two profound events happen so close together in his life, and at such a young age.

Upon my homecoming, we tried to pick up where we had left off. But he was injured, and I was injured, and neither of us had the resources to help the other. He'd moved out of his mom's house and into the dorm at his college, and now I was the one visiting him. We'd see each other on the weekends, and soon our arguments started to escalate. We'd fight, but I would stay through Sunday as planned. Sometimes he'd look at the clock and say, "You gotta leave now."

"OK," I'd say, throwing my stuff in my bag. "I'm leaving."

"No, I mean you gotta leave NOW," he'd yell, practically shoving me out the door. Or he would literally shove me out the door. I'm sure that he had someone else coming around, but back then I didn't want to see it, even though his college buddies would say, out of earshot of Matt, "I don't think you should be with him. He's a scumbag."

I'd return home with bruises or scratches, which became harder to hide. "My brother's a scumbag," Matt's sister would say to me. "I really think you should break up with him." Many of my friends begged me to end it—they even held an intervention. My mother told me I had to stop seeing him. I answered her by breaking our coffee table.

In retrospect—and maybe I'm making excuses—we both needed help, we were both looking for something that we could not give each other. He took his pain out on me; I submitted to it. We both thought we could go back to before and make it all go away. Which, of course, we couldn't.

When I found out he had hurt Savannah, though, that was enough. His hitting me? That was one thing. His treatment of me wasn't much different from how I treated myself, or how I felt I deserved to be treated. But after Savannah had spent a weekend with him and come home with a crooked tail, that was it. There was no way I would let my dog suffer any more than she already had.

It is difficult for me to write about that era. I don't like the person I became after the rape. There was a lot of pretending going on, and I was chasing my pain away with one distraction after another. I got a job as a cocktail waitress at Rumours, a nightclub on the Canadian side of Niagara Falls, where booze and men were always at the ready. I was like a kid in a candy store—money, men, and alcohol coming at me from every direction.

The question I am most often asked when I speak at college campuses is what my relationship with men was like after the assault. At first, this was a hard question for me to answer. It has become easier with time. I recognize that the answer to this question is helpful to others and is certainly something I would have wondered myself. Every survivor has a different answer. In my case, the first thing I did was stay too long in an abusive relationship. Then I decided that I would no longer be a victim. I would no longer be the prey. *I'm the predator here,* I'd think as another man threw himself at me. I just wanted to be a one-dimensional character, to bury the pain and live only on the surface of things. I believed that I could fill the empty chasm that now lived inside me with men, the theory being that if I messed around enough, the man who raped me would just be one of many, his invisible handprints on my body overlaid by the handprints of so many others. I didn't have to worry about anyone but myself; I could treat everyone like crap, and anyone who had a problem with it could go to hell.

I drank. A lot. I woke up in places I didn't recognize, with strangers passed out next to me, my lipstick smeared on their pillows and the smell of beer and vomit in the air. *Holy shit,* I thought the morning I woke up between two guys whose names I couldn't remember or had never learned.

Now, I don't want to sound like I'm disparaging this lifestyle. If that's your thing, then that's your thing, and you'll find no judgment here. You do you, as they say. For me, though, all that messing around wasn't filling me up—in fact, it was making me feel emptier. It just wasn't *me.*

During that time, per usual, I'd fly home to St. Catharines for Thanksgiving and Christmas with my mom and the Osgans. I was always overjoyed to see them, and for the time that I was there I could act like everything was OK. If they noticed something different about me, they didn't say anything, or perhaps they were too busy pretending not to see the state that Vaughn Jr. was in.

He and I were still as close as we'd always been, and even though he was a handsome hetero guy, I trusted him beyond a shadow of a doubt. Like his dad, he was smart and he thrived in school. He'd managed to get crazy off-the-chart scores on the MCAT and PCAT, had graduated from the University of Toronto Department of Pharmacology and Toxicology, at the top of his class, and had gotten a great job as a pharmacist. Vaughn was nothing less than the epitome of conventional success. And yet, it was quite obvious during Christmas dinner of 1995 that he was high as hell. At the dining room table, in front of everyone, his eyes were rolling back in his head, and he was acting straight-up crazy. If I could see it—I might have been an alcohol expert by then, but I'd never gotten into drugs—then surely his parents could see it, too.

They could not. A couple nights before I planned to leave, Mom and I sat them down.

"I don't know how to say this," I said, "so I'm just going to say it. We think Vaughn Jr. is using drugs."

A pregnant pause. Mom and I glanced at each other.

"I agree with Natasha," Mom said. "He's been acting really strange. I think he's on something."

Another pause.

"We appreciate your concern," Vaugh Sr. finally said. "But I have to say that you're wrong. It's just that he's been working so hard. I agree, he seems a little off. But really, that's all it is."

"How could you even think that?" Lucy, Vaughn Jr.'s mom, said, her voice one octave higher than usual. "He's been there for you all these years, and now you're accusing him of taking drugs? You should be ashamed of yourself."

So that didn't go well. I couldn't help beating myself up over it. After all, who was I to judge? I'd ushered in the New Year about as drunk as I'd ever been, and I'd kept up with it ever since.

There was no way I could sustain the life I was living—I was either headed to rock bottom or I'd have to start the climb back up. After a night of epic partying, followed by a few things I'm not proud of, I found myself unable to shake the feeling that I had become someone I despised. I couldn't bear to look at myself in the mirror. I was faced with two choices: I could continue to punish myself, or I could try to find some sort of way to redeem myself. I had to stop blaming myself for what had happened to me, to forgive myself for all the bad choices

I had made. Just because I couldn't describe my rapist didn't mean that it was my fault he wasn't in jail. Just because he'd hurt me didn't mean that I deserved it.

There was no avoiding it anymore—if I wanted to feel better, I was going to have to dig deeper. Back then I took for granted the resources I had at my disposal. I didn't realize how fortunate I was to have a mother who believed me. Through my mother's job I had access to therapy; participation was even encouraged. The therapy I received was not a cure by any means, but it gave me tools that I continue to use to this day.

I also searched for solace in books, something outside of myself I could cling to. I read every religious text I could get my hands on. At first I focused on what I knew—books on Christianity and the Bible. But it wasn't long before I realized that the Bible, or rather, certain interpretations of it, just wasn't sitting right anymore, what with my gay friends and all. I wanted something more "real," something, anything, that would anchor me, or would pull me up from rock bottom, something that would connect me with a higher power that loved me and could help me learn to love myself. I collected books on Buddhism, metaphysics, transcendental meditation. *The Celestine Prophecy* was popular at the time and was blowing everyone's minds. I discovered Richard Bach. I spoke to priests, visited with monks, and did a lot of meditating. I called on my childhood friends Tanya Bhandari and Elana Benson. We're still close, and we still talk about the same things we did back then—what's going on in our lives, what we believe in, why we are doing the things that we're doing.

I did everything I could to face the woman who'd materialized from the ashes of my assault.

In 1996 I met a nice boy named Jeff Ning, fell in love, and moved to Florida.

You know that saying "Wherever you go, there you are"? It's absolutely true. No matter how much moving I did, I couldn't escape the post-rape Natasha. In Florida, every time I'd make some progress, that Natasha would show up and crash my party.

On occasion, I'd receive mug shots of suspects in the mail. While there would sometimes be a tiny similarity to the man that attacked me here or there, I was never comfortable picking out someone. I just didn't trust my memory, and I had a lot of guilt about it. To be honest, even after all that soul-searching, I still blamed myself for the entire event. I wished I could say something specific (though completely and absolutely untrue) like, "Well, I shouldn't have been walking alone that late at night." But there wasn't any particular detail I could reasonably take the blame for—it was just a feeling, so *unspecific* that it was more like "It's my fault because I am me."

This was the late nineties, years before scholars like Dr. Rebecca Campbell talked about the neurobiology of trauma and how stress hormones can affect our memory.[9] I just felt like something was wrong with me. And when I was told that they were closing my case due to lack of leads, my heart broke. I knew my rapist was out there harming others, and that it was entirely my fault.

Around that time, I met someone with whom I had a lot in common. He had just returned from Iraq, and we were both in so much pain and unequipped to deal with it. He seemed to be the only one around who *got* me. And so I left the nice boy I'd moved to Florida with for the badass veteran.

I think we were good for each other in the beginning. We moved in together in Ormond Beach, several miles away from my new job in the Special Events Department at Daytona International Speedway. I was never a race fan and never became one, but I certainly appreciated the sportsmanship of the game.

---

9. Rebecca Campbell, "The Neurobiology of Sexual Assault," December 3, 2012, transcript and recording, National Institute of Justice, https://nij.gov/multimedia/presenter/presenter-campbell/pages/presenter-campbell-transcript.aspx.

It was 1998 and 124,000 acres of northeast Florida, including Ormond Beach, were engulfed in flames.[10] A mandatory evacuation was ordered as the wildfires made headway toward our residential area. I took everything I could carry and, with my mom, who was visiting at the time, went to stay with my boss, Marsha.

The Daytona International team had all been working diligently to prepare the track for the Pepsi 400, which was supposed to be the largest sports night ever in Speedway history. Because of poor visibility due to smoke, John Graham, president of the Speedway, decided to postpone the race just two days before it was supposed to begin. To their credit, the Speedway owners jumped into action to aid the displaced families. The food that had initially been prepared for race fans was served to victims of the fire and the amazing fire fighters who were keeping us safe. The entire special events team was out there every day handing out food and water to those in need. It didn't take long for President Bill Clinton to notice us in our Florida inferno.

On July 9, 1998, I met William Jefferson Clinton. This was in the midst of his sex scandal. That morning, in reference to the photo of him embracing his former intern, which was being flashed on television stations across the nation, my mother joked, "Don't hug him!"

President Clinton met with a group of us in a tent just outside the main Speedway venue. He had a charisma like no one I'd ever seen. When he stepped up to the podium to speak, I couldn't take my eyes off of him; he had us all hypnotized as he gave a very moving address before stepping off the stage to approach the crowd.

Marsha and I were the only women not in uniform, and we snuck our way to the very front of the room to get a better look at the president. He stopped in front of me, then put his left arm around my shoulders and stayed like that as he shook everyone's hand one by one.

---

10. http://www.nytimes.com/1998/07/04/us/florida-county-evacuated-on-fear-of-merged-fires.html

Marsha gasped, disposable camera at the ready, and took photo after photo. There was nothing odd about the exchange if you were there to see it. It was very formal, actually. But after my mother's directive, it was pretty funny.

Around that time, out of the blue, I received a letter.

I won't replicate it verbatim here. If I wanted to do that, I'd have to call my mom, who has the shredded-and-then-taped-back-together paper tucked away somewhere. The gist of it was this: "I hope that your rape didn't turn you into a prude . . . I want to pleasure you in every orifice. Sincerely, Vaughn Sr."

Recalling those words makes me feel nauseated all over again. For unknowable reasons, Vaughn Sr., a man I'd known almost all my life, whose son was like a brother to me, had decided that now, at twenty-five, I was old enough to solicit. His letter brought back some memories of his telling me that women weren't worthwhile after twenty-five, so perhaps he'd decided to make his play before I aged out of sexual attractiveness. He'd given me lots of other stellar nuggets of wisdom, such as men don't want to have sex with women while on their period and that women are inherently dirty. These are the kinds of things you don't think about as a kid, because when someone who's like a father to you says them, then that must just be the way it is.

But the letter was something else entirely. I was absolutely astonished, angry, heartsick. I tore it up and burst into tears, the kind of tears that turn into sobs that turn into howls, a show of emotion I rarely made. I must have scared my veteran boyfriend, because later he went through the trash and found all the paper shreds, taped them back together, read the letter, and then mailed it to my mom. He knew that I'd probably end up forgiving Vaughn Sr., but that my mom would never, ever let it go.

And she hasn't. When she received that letter in the mail, she freaked out. After all, Vaughan Sr. had betrayed her, too—she'd trusted him with me, and she'd been so glad that he could fill in the space that my biological father had left in my life. Mom had a book she'd borrowed from him; she returned it, with a copy of the letter inside and a note at the top that said, "Natasha will never speak to you again, and here's why."

Suffice it to say that that event destroyed our relationship. To cover his tracks, Vaughn Sr. began to bad-mouth me to his family, Vaughn Jr. in particular, creating a rift that we've yet to cross. Later, when he and his wife found their son passed out on the floor of their bathroom and finally admitted to themselves the extent of his drug problem, Vaughn Sr. blamed me, saying that it had gone so far because I'd known about it and hadn't put a stop to it, that I'd enabled him. Vaughn Sr. forgot to mention that Christmastime conversation we'd had years earlier. This became the excuse for our families' estrangement, rather than the fact that he wrote his almost-daughter a highly sexual letter five years after her rape.

Losing Vaughn Jr. has been really hard for me. Not only was he a heterosexual man who'd never hit on me, but during the early days after the rape, when I felt crazy and alone and was acting out, he was the one who could pull me back down to earth. He'd also planted the seed of feminism in my mind. The apple *did* fall far from the tree in that respect—he believed in the equality of women and men. He is why, all these years later, I can look back at Vaughn Sr. with feminist eyes and see his misogyny and how mixed up he was about women and sex. Rape isn't sex, sex isn't rape. Why would rape affect my sexuality? Also, why wouldn't it? Either way, it was none of his goddamn business.

Vaughn Sr. was no Victor Rondon, the man I'd later learn was my attacker; that's easy to see. But perhaps both men view women as objects, as less than, and not as living, breathing, feeling people. Both used manipulation to get what they wanted—in Victor Rondon's case, a gun was his tool of manipulation; Vaughn Sr. used coercion, secrecy, and shame.

I've heard through the grapevine that Vaughn Jr. has recovered and now works to help other medical professionals who find themselves suffering with addiction. I hope he's well. I have also, like my veteran boyfriend predicted, forgiven Vaughn Sr. Friends of mine say to me, "You got to stop forgiving people." But that's just what I do.

My life at the Daytona Speedway didn't last for much longer. While they treated me quite well, my heart just wasn't in it. I wanted to do more—I wanted to make a difference, like I had helping those families in the fire.

I'd been following People for the Ethical Treatment of Animals since I was in high school. While browsing their website one day, back when images took what felt like years to load, I stumbled upon a job listing. I immediately sent my resume and a cover letter. I was called in for two interviews and eventually offered a job at their headquarters in Norfolk, Virginia. And so my Iraq War veteran boyfriend and I moved our lives and our dogs to Hampton Roads.

It was 2000 and I was thrilled to be working for PETA. I became a vegan and began meditating again. I felt good, like I was making a difference in the world. The staff had incredible dedication to the cause, and being a PETA employee was like attending a nonprofit boot camp. I learned all the ins and outs, soon discovering that I didn't agree with all of the organization's tactics. Quick quiz: Do you know PETA's advertising budget? It's zero dollars, zero cents. Yet you've heard of them, right? That's a feat in itself, whether you like the organization or not.

Sadly, PETA and I were all wrong for each other.

I got a new job at the Mariners' Museum in Newport News as the manager of special events. My boss, Karen Price, was always impeccably dressed and had a wealth of knowledge on just about everything. She was a strong and savvy businesswoman whom I wanted to emulate in every way.

The museum felt like home to me, and I really enjoyed my job and the company of the interesting and intelligent staff. For the first time since I'd moved back to the United States, I felt like I belonged somewhere. No one knew about the rape, and I liked it that way very much. I came into work every day and just did my thing, confident that I was good at it. Unfortunately, things were not going so well at home.

My boyfriend and I had begun to self-medicate, alcohol being our medicine of choice. Our tender, honest moments were now few and far between. Instead, vicious arguments had become a regular thing. It was pretty clear that we didn't like each other anymore, but for some reason we held on to each other for dear life. We were a lot alike in many ways, including our unaddressed self-loathing. I wish I could say that we woke up one day, looked at each other, and exclaimed in perfect unison, "We both have posttraumatic stress disorder! Now let's get some help!"

That didn't happen. It's so much easier to pretend everything is OK. We were both able to hold down jobs; so what if we drank a little too much, got a little out of control now and again? I'd found solace in playing video games, through which I could escape to distant lands where I was strong, and I could win, and if I got hurt, I could just press the reset button.

Between video games and work I had plenty to keep my mind busy. For a while I was able to forget the mess that was going on in my relationship. I didn't think much about the rape, or at least I didn't think I did. I thought I'd made peace with the fact that we'd never find the man who assaulted me. What I couldn't shake was my gnawing guilt. *If I was a better witness, this monster wouldn't be free,* I'd think as I splashed water on my face after waking up in a cold sweat and running to the bathroom to vomit. The guilt was slowly destroying me, devouring me from the inside out. I didn't tell anyone what was happening to me. Not even my mother.

Rape, like many other crimes, affects everyone connected to the victim. I cannot even imagine what it would be like as a mother to know your daughter had been violated in such a way. Mom and I were close, yet we didn't discuss how we were dealing with the aftershock of it all. It was a lot easier to assume that we had both moved on. It only *almost* came up when I got my HIV test results every six months. I would call her and say, "It's negative again, Mom."

Praise God, she'd say back.

Every December I returned home to Canada for the holidays. I felt I was doing a pretty good job of hiding my fear and pain. My mom and I never spoke of the assault, and we didn't tell anyone in our immediate family. And while I, at least, had a handful of friends that were aware of what happened, my mother had no one. I don't know how she managed all those years.

To keep our secret, we explained why I'd left New York in a number of ways. I told some people that I missed my mom too much, and to others I said that I'd run out of money. I often claimed that it was because I'd changed my major to veterinary medicine. My favorite fib, however, was that someone in my building had gotten mugged, and after that I was too afraid to stay in New York. Whatever the reason I gave, it was painful for me when people responded with, "We knew you'd be back." So while coming home to visit Mom was fulfilling, a lot of energy still went into hiding and telling lies and dealing with the reaction. I was happy most of the time, but the pretending was just exhausting.

Back in Virginia, I'd settle back into my routine of going to work, playing video games, and ignoring the enormous pink PTSD elephant in the room. Of course, PTSD only gets worse if you don't treat it. My life was slowly spiraling out of control, and my relationship was reaching a breaking point. How could we possibly be able to fix it, when both of us were falling apart?

Now, often I would wake up in the middle of the night to find his hands wrapped around my throat. The first time it happened, I roused him easily, and we both sort of shrugged it off. As time went on, however, the strangling became a nightly occurrence, and it became harder for me to wake him up. To make certain he didn't accidentally kill me in the middle of the night, he moved to a different bedroom. Why we thought that was the best option is beyond me.

With both of us sinking deeper and deeper into despair, neither he nor I had the power to stop what was happening or the wherewithal to ask for help. No one had a clue as to what was going on.

My boyfriend and I never talked about marriage or starting a family. Such conversations would've required resources and a hope in the future that we just didn't have. We stayed together for nearly six years before we came up for air.

He was, however, there when the call came.

4.

GAME CHANGER

"What comes around, goes around."
—Mom

It was a balmy February day in 2003 when I got a voice mail from the New York County District Attorney's Office. I immediately knew what it was about.

I remember exactly where I was when I finally spoke to Melissa Mourges, assistant district attorney and chief of the Forensic Sciences/Cold Case Unit in the New York County District Attorney's Office. I still dream about that house in Newport News, Virginia. Built just after the turn of the twentieth century, like the others in the Hilton Village neighborhood, it was all brick, with no driveways or closets but tons of character. Every room was painted a different color, with crown molding and those old doors with the crystal doorknobs that turn opaque from age. What I loved the most about that house was its library—yes, a real library, with built-in, floor-to-ceiling bookshelves.

I was standing in the kitchen, surrounded by walls painted a buttery yellow. This was before I had a cell phone, and I'd wrapped the wall phone's cord around my finger. Outside the big southwest-facing windows, beyond the porch and the yard, the James River flowed slowly by.

"We tested your rape kit," Melissa told me.

"What do you mean?" I asked, confused.

Of course they'd tested my rape kit, hadn't they? I mean . . . I went through all that, when all I'd wanted was a hot shower. They wouldn't have made me go through that for no reason, right?

Turned out, my rape kit had been sitting in a county storage facility collecting dust for nearly a decade. Everything it contained—my underwear, my fingernail scrapings, the perpetrator's DNA—had been sealed up, untouched for all that time. I couldn't believe it.

Back then, there was a statute of limitations on the crime of rape in New York. After ten years my perpetrator could walk into a police department, slap a stack of photos of the crime down on the counter, say, "I raped this woman," and walk out a free man. Can you imagine? (In 2006, New York State removed the statute of limitations on rape.[11])

Ms. Mourges wanted me to come to New York and testify before a grand jury so that we could charge the DNA in the rape kit with the crime. This would stop the clock on that statute of limitations. While there was yet to be a match for the DNA in CODIS, the national Combined DNA Index System, there might be, one day.

I'm often asked if I was angry when I received that phone call. In truth, I was more surprised than anything—I had no idea I had cause to be angry. Almost every night for eight years I'd woken up in a cold sweat and vomited, the guilt about not remembering what my attacker

---

11. William J. Larkin, Jr., "Senate Passes Legislation To Eliminate Statue of Limitations For Rape Victims," news release, June 22, 2006, https://www.nysenate.gov/newsroom/press-releases/william-j-larkin-jr/senate-passes-legislation-eliminate-statute-limitations.

looked like overwhelming me. So in that moment, all I could feel was gratitude. Maybe the fact that my rapist hadn't been apprehended wasn't my fault after all.

What I didn't know was that my rape kit was just one of nearly 17,000 unprocessed rape kits in New York City,[12] each containing the story of a victim whose body was a crime scene, just like mine. It wasn't that the New York State Division of Criminal Justice Services didn't care about those kits. The issue was New York City had yet to connect with CODIS, and therefore, even if they'd processed all those kits, they wouldn't have been able to access the necessary information.

CODIS is like a fingerprint database, only DNA is what's recorded. There are two parts to CODIS: crime scene evidence and DNA profiles. Crime scene evidence, like that found in rape kits, is uploaded into the crime scene portion of the database in the hopes that it will match an identity stored in the profile portion of the database. Without a connection to the national database, there really is no way (that can be used in a court of law) to find a match to DNA left at a crime scene.

In 2000, New York City joined CODIS, allowing the city to clear its 17,000-kit backlog at a cost of nearly $12 million.[13] Every single kit was cleared from the shelf and sent off for testing at private labs across the nation. My rape kit was one of those kits. Class of 2003!

Today, I speak at the Special Victims Division training sessions on a regular basis, and I'm fortunate enough to know many police officers in the NYPD. In New York City, officers must volunteer to be on the Special Victims Division. Believe it or not, many police departments across the country assign police officers to that unit as a form of punishment.

---

12. http://manhattanda.org/ending-national-rape-kit-backlog
13. http://www.endthebacklog.org/new-york-city

All the NYPD officers who work in sex crimes have told me the same thing—testing kits makes their job easier. If a perp is already in the system, they get a warrant and make an arrest. This means that a serial rapist—of which there are many—caught in New York could be linked to the other crimes he's committed across the country through his DNA. It's just that simple.

The day after talking to Assistant DA Mourges, I told my boss, Karen, the whole story. That in 1993 I'd been raped at gunpoint and the perpetrator had never been found. That all these years later, the DA's office had called me to testify before the grand jury. I asked Karen for time off and begged her not to tell anyone why I was leaving. At that point, I was going to visit my grandmother in Long Island so often that I don't think anyone even bothered to ask about my absence.

Returning to New York gave me an opportunity to see the city again and spend time with Trevor, who'd stayed put there after high school and had become a very successful fashion designer. I was also looking forward to seeing my paternal grandmother, Babushka, who was, day by day, slipping into the impassable world of dementia. My half sister, Kathryn (we have the same father), was staying with her while we figured out what to do next. I'd been traveling to Long Island every other week to check in on how they were doing, but not once had I ventured back into the city—I hadn't been ready yet. Now I was going there with a purpose: to tell my story before a grand jury.

I splurged on a room at the Waldorf Astoria. As teenagers, Kathryn and I had often gone to the hotel to sit in the lobby and discreetly watch the people checking in. We'd make up stories about their lives, and often much-older men would approach us and invite us to their rooms. We'd just giggle and run away.

My relationship with my half sister has always been intense. I was twelve years old when we met for the first time, four years after our father's death. At seventeen, Kathryn was everything I wanted to be.

She was tiny and graceful, while I was awkward and gangly. She looked like a doll, with her gigantic blue eyes and a mane of lovely blonde hair. She'd never had the chance to get to know our father, and I was far too young to recognize how difficult that must have been for her. I grew up thinking Kathryn hung the moon.

For a while, I tried to copy her in everything, from the clothing she wore to the music she listened to, and she wrote me weekly letters and sent me care packages filled with "big girl" things. But as the years passed, a rift developed between us. She had won a scholarship for graduate school in Russia, and she'd returned hooked on opiates. Around the time I was recovering from my assault, she was recovering from drug addiction. Babushka and my mother tried to keep us apart, afraid that, in my fragile state, I too might succumb to the same disease. I wasn't there for her during her struggles, and, frankly, I wouldn't have been of any help. Now, all these years later, we were working on rebuilding our relationship, and I was excited about getting the chance to spend time with her, however nonideal the reason.

I met Melissa—Assistant DA Mourges—in a small courthouse downtown, an old building that reminded me of a school. The halls were narrow, the only sounds the clicking of heels and the occasional buzzing of a fluorescent light bulb. Melissa walked very quickly, and I tried to keep up with her pace. She meant business; you could tell by her very aura. At first I was so intimidated I couldn't even look her in the eye.

We went into a small room, where the procedure for giving grand jury testimony was explained to me. I would go into the courtroom, swear on the Bible, and tell everyone exactly what happened to me on August 6, 1993. What sticks in my mind the most was the moment when Melissa told me that I had to say *penis* and *vagina* and not any other word. She also explained that I would have to share every gruesome detail, to clearly describe where he put his penis and when. While I couldn't remember his face, I did remember each act very clearly. I also remembered the gun with such clarity that, even to this day, when I shut my eyes I can see every inch of it.

I don't remember my exact testimony to the grand jury. I remember answering Melissa's questions, and I remember hearing someone sobbing. Maybe it was me sobbing, though I can't say for certain. Sometimes trauma plays tricks like that.

When it was over, and it was over quickly, Melissa thanked me for coming and told me about a grant they'd received that had helped pay to have the kits tested. I asked her what would happen next.

"One of two things usually happen in these cases," she began in her usual authoritative tone. "We find the perps when they go to or leave prison, or we don't find them because they are dead."

A chill ran down my spine. I had some answers to questions that had plagued me for years, plus a very nice and skilled assistant DA believed in me. I knew that we still might never find the man who raped me—since there was no match, he was either dead or in jail, where he couldn't hurt anyone. I tried not to think too much about the possibility that he might be somewhere out there, his DNA forever free and uncatalogued. Instead, I had to take this minor victory for what it was. I would take anything at that point.

"Here's the deal, Mom," I said without bothering to say hello. I'd rushed out of the building to call her on my new cell phone and tell her the news. "If we don't find him he's either dead or in jail. If he's not in jail, we'll find him eventually. Isn't that great news?" That wasn't *exactly* what Melissa had said, but it was close enough.

After giving my testimony, I returned to Long Island with my sister to discuss our grandmother's future. We had to face the fact that things had taken a turn for the worse. Neither of us wanted to put her in a home, so we agreed that, for the time being, Kathryn would take care of her. She wasn't sure how much longer she could stay with our grandmother; my sister had more than enough on her plate.

I couldn't blame her one bit. The house was falling to pieces. A majority of the windows were cracked, and the siding was peeling off in sheets. The grass was so high you could get lost in it. Prior to our arrival, our grandmother had been using the floor as a toilet. But it was Babushka's house, and we knew it meant everything to her.

I returned to Virginia with a heavy heart, knowing full well that I wouldn't be there much longer.

It's really hard to concentrate on any one thing when thoughts are racing through your head faster than you can find places for them to land. I had to deal with my boyfriend the midnight strangler, my grandmother the crazy Russian, and Natasha the rape victim, who was coming closer to getting justice. Was there room for all of these characters in my life?

Life has a funny way of making decisions for you when you can't make your own. My sister called me to tell me she was pregnant. Obviously, my soon-to-be nephew would have to come first.

In early 2004, I quit my job, broke up with my boyfriend, and moved in with my grandmother in Long Island. My sister went home to Minnesota.

My rape kit had been tested and my rapist was either dead, in jail, or, hopefully, soon to be caught. For the first time since I could remember, anything was possible. The house was falling down around me, my grandmother's dementia was worsening, but I had a new lease on life. I would be the best granddaughter the world had ever seen. I would take the best care of my babushka, and if I loved her enough, maybe her memory would improve and she'd remember who I was. Maybe I would remember who I was, too.

With all that change going on in my life, it didn't take long for old habits to reemerge. I had all this new, raw emotion, and I couldn't bring myself to use the coping tools I'd learned in therapy and in books, the tools that had always brought me to a better place. Because of the severity of Babushka's dementia, I couldn't leave her alone for any length of time, so further therapy wasn't an option. I did hire a contractor to make the house safer; at the very least we needed to fix the ceilings before they fully caved in. In retrospect, putting a ninety-year-old woman suffering from dementia in the care of a rape survivor with untreated PTSD probably wasn't the greatest idea.

Not that our time together didn't have beauty or meaning—it did. Babushka loved John Travolta, in particular his slicked-back-hair character in the musical *Grease*. I bought the DVD and put it on repeat all day, every day, for her enjoyment. I cannot tell you how many times she rushed up to me and said, as though for the first time, "Natasha! *Grease* is on! John Travolta! Come see!" Then she'd sway back and forth and clap her hands, with a look on her face that said, *I'm dancing and I shouldn't be. Aren't I naughty?*

I kid you not; my ninety-year-old Russian babushka had moves.

Sadly, for every Danny Zuko–inspired moment of joy, there were a hundred moments of strain. Once again, my mother saved the day. She knew that my living situation wasn't healthy for me or for my grandmother. And so she found a lovely nursing home for Babushka, located just around the corner from Mom's place in St. Catharines, which we could afford because of the money Babushka had squirreled away. One of my good friends from high school worked there as a nurse, and my mother promised she would visit Babushka at least every other day—a promise she kept.

My grandmother moved, and I remained behind in Long Island to figure out what to do with her house.

I wouldn't be able to delay the inevitable for very much longer. I'd used taking care of my grandmother as an excuse for not taking care of myself. To not look myself in the eye and say, *Natasha, hold on a sec. Just process everything that has happened over the last few years.*

I preferred to still go along like everything was fine. It was better, though, and that's the truth. So the years passed very quickly, and I stayed in my grandmother's house. My intention had been to fix it up and rent it so that Babushka's increasingly expensive nursing home bills would always be covered. But Savannah, my new dog, a vizsla named Zoë, and I were enjoying the acres of land and the lack of responsibility too much to let it go. To maintain our little hideaway, I took a job as a marketing and public relations manager at a company where I'd be exposed for the first time to a truly toxic work environment. But it paid really well. And though the outside of the house was a disaster, the inside was shaping up nicely, and it was beginning to fill up with good memories. Plus Islip was this charming little mom-and-pop kind of town. The downtown area was straight out of the 1950s—old, two-story buildings, no chains or big-name retail or restaurants to speak of. Like a Norman Rockwell painting, but with a healthy multicultural and multigenerational mix of people, and close to the city. I think that, in my heart, my intention had always been to stay.

While on vacation in Canada toward the end of summer in 2007, I received a phone call from my neighbor in Long Island. Every day for a week, she reported, a blue sedan had parked in front of the house. The driver, a man in a suit, sat there all day taking notes. It was creepy.

For whatever reason, I thought I was in trouble for something. Had I done anything to warrant that conclusion? Absolutely not, but that is how my mind operates, always jumping right to the worst possible scenario.

I cut my vacation short and hurried back to Long Island to figure out who was spying on me. The afternoon after my return, there was a knock at the door. I felt my heart pounding as I answered it.

"I'm looking for Natasha Alexenko?" the man in the suit said, obviously nervous.

"Hi. I'm Natasha," I answered.

"Um, there was something bad that happened in 1993?" he stammered. "Well, call this lady in the New York DA's office; she has news for you."

My hands took on a life of their own. They trembled as I covered my face so that he would not see the expression I was making. I think, though I can't be sure, that I was smiling.

He handed me a business card and left. That was it. To be honest, I kind of found his nervousness endearing. He was a human being, after all. It couldn't be easy to deliver that type of news, in person, face to face.

After calling the number on the card to no avail, I called my mother to tell her the news.

"Mom, I think they found him." I didn't have to say which *him* I was speaking of.

"You don't know for sure yet, so don't get your hopes up," she said.

I didn't hear back from Assistant DA Melissa Mourges that day, and I found myself beginning to panic. What if she was trying to contact me because *he* had found me? What if he was out there, headed toward me? I dove into the bed, pulled the covers over my head, and started to cry. Savannah had died the year before, and I wanted her desperately. I knew she would lick away my tears and make me laugh, if only she were next to me. Fortunately Zoë had inherited Savannah's strong, stoic nature. She stood watch over me while I cried.

After several hours of terror, I decided to call my local rape crisis center. Surely they had an answer to my many questions, the right words to soothe me and calm me down. At this point, I was crying so hard I could barely breathe.

I told the rape crisis volunteer my whole story, how I was raped on August 6, 1993, and that my rape kit had gone untested for nearly a decade. I described my encounter with the nice nervous man in the suit, and told her about my panic and my fear of what this all meant.

Her answer was chilling: "It's 2007, though. Why are you calling all upset about something that happened such a long time ago?"

I hung up the phone, drove to the store, and bought a bottle of wine.

When I tell the story of that phone call in the presence of rape crisis teams, there is *always* an audible gasp. Generally, rape crisis hotlines are staffed with some of the most caring, most dedicated people in the world. My dear friends at the Rape, Abuse and Incest National Network (RAINN) have a national hotline and a private online chat feature, and their volunteers can connect survivors to the right people in their jurisdiction. The number is 1-800-656-HOPE or chat online at www.RAINN.org.[14]

It took a few days to get ahold of Melissa. It was raining when I took her call.

"Natasha, I hope you're sitting down," she began. "We found the man that raped you in 1993."

I wasn't sitting down. I was at my terrible marketing job, and I'd had to wind my way through a field of cubicles, with everyone giving me the stink-eye as I went by. Taking personal calls during working hours was just not acceptable. But obviously this could not wait, and now I was standing outside where no one could overhear my conversation. And I didn't care that it was raining anymore.

"Is he in jail? Does he know where I live?" I asked desperately.

"You are safe, Natasha," Melissa said. "He's behind bars."

A flood of relief washed over me. And, I kid you not, the rain abruptly stopped that very minute, like someone had shut off the tap. It was absolutely quiet, and petrichor, that earthy smell after water hits dry soil, filled my nostrils as I took a deep breath. There's really no better smell in the world.

---

14. https://www.rainn.org/about-rainn

Melissa's words filled me with a sense of well-being. At least I assumed that was what I was feeling—it had been so long since I'd felt that way that I didn't quite remember what well-being felt like. Simultaneously, I was filled with a sense of urgency—I had to know the answer to a question that had plagued me for years, an answer that would give me some of my power back. I needed someone at whom to direct my anger.

"What is his name?"

"His name is Victor Perfect Rondon," she said.

I thanked her profusely. She told me that he was locked away and would remain so until a plea bargain was reached, or a court date was set. She promised I would hear from her soon.

So what had Victor Rondon been doing for all those years?

Well, he'd been on a nationwide, one-man crime spree. Shortly after I was raped, Victor Rondon was caught with the 9mm semiautomatic weapon he had used on me. He was carrying it illegally, and he went to jail for a few years before being released on parole. Apparently Victor Rondon decided he'd had enough of victimizing people in New York, so he traveled to different states across the country, selling crack, women, and handguns. Every time he got arrested, he used a different name, so no one knew he was in violation of parole. Victor Rondon made his way to Las Vegas, Nevada, where he was finally arrested. Can you guess what he was arrested for in Sin City, where the regular rules don't apply?

Victor Rondon was busted for, of all things, jaywalking. When the officer handed the citation over, Victor Rondon decided to assault him. He was promptly taken into custody, where he was booked and fingerprinted. Then the police extradited him to New York for violating his parole. Finally, his bad deeds had caught up with him.

I have met the NYPD detective who swabbed Victor Rondon's cheek for the DNA that would eventually be uploaded into CODIS. He's my hero. On August 6, 2007, exactly fourteen years *to the day* after

I was raped, Victor Rondon's name replaced the name "John Doe" on my rape kit. His DNA matched that which had been found at the crime scene, my body.

As most people are well aware, trials take a while. I had no idea that they took that long—arrest to arraignment can take months, if not years. The wait for this trial felt even longer, though our court date was set at April 2008. Timing wasn't great—I was just about to start a new job at the Long Island Maritime Museum. This was going to prove awkward. How would I tell my new boss what I was about to go through? Simple: I just didn't.

Trevor and my friend Damon came with me to the courthouse that April morning. Melissa met us there. You know when you care about someone so much that they become absolutely, almost otherworldly, beautiful to you? That's what Melissa looks like to me.

I hadn't slept the night before, but that was nothing new. I was both nervous and confident, and I had the utmost confidence in Melissa. We had many years of trust-building behind us—she'd even driven to my house to find me and didn't say word one about its derelict state. I believed in her, and she believed in me. We were going to put this man away, where he would never hurt anyone ever again.

Cilia Crisp, my long-ago roommate and friend, was also there to greet me at the courthouse. I hadn't seen her in over fourteen years. She looked exactly the same, with her wheat-colored hair and light-brown eyes, the freckles dotting her delicate features in exactly the same places they had in 1993. We embraced. I was sad that it had taken so long for us to see each other again.

She and I caught up in the waiting room. Jimmy (now her ex) didn't want to come to the trial, unable to bear going through all that again. Another woman whom Victor Rondon tried to assault the same night he assaulted me didn't want to come to court, either. We wouldn't be hearing from all the people he'd victimized in the last fifteen years—this trial was about my rape only, and in essence we'd be pretending that it was still 1993.

Cilia took the stand before me. I waited, both relaxed and tense, knowing I was going to finally be empowered to tell the truth. Then it was my turn.

I walked slowly into the courtroom. I tried not to look at the jurors, but I could feel their eyes on me as I passed the jury box and moved toward the stand. The chair, where I would sit and give my testimony and finally be heard, loomed up ahead. Then I saw Victor Perfect Rondon out of the corner of my eye.

In that moment, the chair, the jurors, the entire courtroom vanished, and the person of Victor Rondon emerged into perfect focus. I felt as though I was being hurled back through the space-time continuum to August 6, 1993. My logical mind knew I was safe, but my traumatized animal brain was telling me to get the hell out of there. Once again I felt as though I was trying to breathe in water, my lungs too heavy to get enough air, my legs frozen in place.

Dr. Rebecca Campbell, in her many scientific papers, books, and presentations, describes the neurobiology of trauma and the fight-or-flight response, a term first coined by Walter Bradford Cannon. In the most basic sense, it involves the brain sending a rush of hormones through the body at the first sign of real or perceived danger, in an attempt to protect the organism by prompting it to respond through fighting, fleeing, or freezing.

I was clearly in freeze mode. And then I was in faint mode. Luckily, the bailiff was there to catch me.

I was escorted back to the waiting room, where I chugged at least five glasses of water in quick succession. Trevor later told me that, in all his life, he had never seen a human being drink that much water in one go. I took deep, mindful breaths and began to implement the coping tools I had learned from half a lifetime of trying to heal. I focused on

64

my breathing and allowing my body to relax. I prayed for guidance and strength. Finally, after about twenty minutes, I was ready to try again.

There is something called the rape shield law[15] that prevents crime victims from being traumatized while testifying. Your sex life, what you were wearing, what you were drinking, and other irrelevant private information is not permitted into evidence—that's simply Defense Practices 101. Victor Rondon's lawyer broke that sacred rule right off the bat, asking me straight-out, "Were you a virgin when this happened?"

I don't know any other crime for which its victims are put on trial in this manner. (Or, for that matter, a crime in which the victim has to pay out of pocket for the investigation; sometimes the state charges the victim's health insurance for the rape kit exam!) If someone is murdered in cold blood, no one says, *Well, did you see how he dressed? No wonder the killer got the wrong idea.* If someone is burgled, no one says, *I mean, why would he have all that stuff in the first place? It's like he was asking to get robbed.* If someone gets hit by a drunk driver, no one says, *Yeah, but he was driving, too. So they must both be to blame.* Of course no one says these things—that'd be crazy! In those instances, we would blame the person who committed the crime. The same standards of logic should apply to assault and rape, whether the perpetrator is a stranger, an acquaintance, a friend, or a significant other. Rape is not about sex or undeniable urges; it is violence at its most abhorrent, in which pain and humiliation are the method of domination. And those who rape seek to control—therefore, they are in control of not just their victims but the behavior itself.

I knew not to answer the defense attorney's question. I'm not certain what she was going for there. Perhaps she was trying to shake me,

---

15. "Shield Laws – Rape Shield Laws," accessed July 6, 2017, http://law.jrank.org/pages/10253/Shield-Laws-Rape-Shield-Laws.html

but I wouldn't budge. Instead, I calmly waited for Melissa to object, then went through my entire testimony without a hiccup. I was determined to put my truth out there, to regain control of the situation. It wasn't my fault, it had never been my fault, and I would no longer hold that shame in my heart. The law was on my side, and the truth belonged to me.

I didn't stay to listen to the other testimonies. I didn't stay to hear Victor Rondon add perjury to his rap sheet by saying that we'd met on the subway and I'd gone with him to his apartment, where we'd done cocaine and had consensual sex. I'd also had sex with his roommate, according to him. Thinking back on who I was at twenty, this makes me laugh. I wouldn't have even known what cocaine was if I saw it, and if I did know, I would've cried and run away. The rest of it is not so funny. Nor is the fact that the apartment he claimed we went to actually belonged to his ex-girlfriend, who had taken out a restraining order on him. I wasn't the first woman he'd violated, nor would I be the last. He also, oddly enough, said that his mother was dead. Things got a little awkward when my attorney pointed her out among the other spectators in the gallery.

Melissa called me a short time later—I hadn't even left the city yet.

"Guilty on all eight counts. You're a rock star," she told me.

"Oh, thank God!" I shouted into the phone.

Justice. Good defeated evil, and Victor Perfect Rondon would no longer be free, able to hurt others. I felt my heart beat in my chest, and the city looked more beautiful to me than it ever had before. I cried happy tears, excited to go home and change into my pajamas and tell Zoë the good news.

My mother, absent from the trial for obvious reasons, did come to the sentencing in May of 2008. I read a victim's impact statement to the judge, expressing the pain, fear, and anger that Victor Rondon had caused. I talked about my mother, about how she would never be the same again.

The counts Victor Rondon was convicted of in my case included sodomy, rape, burglary, and sexual abuse. The judge sentenced him to 44 to 107 years behind bars. I watched them take away the monster who'd haunted my nightmares for so many years.

I looked over at my mother and was surprised to find her sobbing.

"It's OK, Mom. It's over. He's gone," I said.

"It's not that," she said between sobs. "He just looks like a decent guy. I was expecting him to look scary."

I don't exactly feel compassion for Victor Rondon, but I don't hate him, either. Holding anger toward him would have destroyed me. The trial and the sentencing were never about revenge; rather, they were about keeping him from harming others. For me, after going through something so difficult and painful, I couldn't just sit by and let the same thing happen to someone else. That's what the trial did for me, but this is my own personal truth and in no way "the rule." To be honest, I didn't get closure from testifying against Victor Rondon on behalf of the people of New York.

But I did become an advocate.

5.

From Survivor to Advocate

"You can be anything you want to be."
—Mom

On the day of the sentencing, standing on the steps of the courthouse, I made a promise to ADA Melissa Mourges. I promised her I would do whatever I could to ensure others received the same justice I had, if that's what they wanted.

"The most important thing you can do, Natasha, is come out as a survivor of sexual assault."

And I did.

Coming forward isn't easy, and I wouldn't say that it's necessarily everyone's calling. I will say, however, that I have never regretted it, not for a millisecond. Offering to come forward threw a tiny spotlight on me for fifteen minutes, and I was invited to work on the HBO documentary *Sex Crimes Unit*.[16]

---

16. *Sex Crimes Unit*, directed by Lisa F. Jackson (2011; USA: HBO)

I never thought in a million years that I would end up in a documentary (and that my underwear would have a role, too). I was fortunate to develop a close relationship with the director, Lisa F. Jackson. Apparently, women actually do make films. She was extremely kind and patient, and she knew when to move forward and when I needed space. We filmed mostly in New York City, and it was the first time in eighteen years that I returned to the scene of the crime. We filmed our interviews in Lisa's apartment, which was just ten blocks from where I used to live on West 95th. The smells of mustard-slathered hot dogs, salted pretzels, and fried samosas from the street vendors took me back in time to when I thought this would be my home forever.

Even though—perhaps because—I adored Lisa, it was sometimes difficult for me to be around her. A successful director, cool and sleek with amazing taste and plenty of adventures to share from her travels around the globe, she was who I'd aspired to be when I'd first moved to New York as a nineteen-year-old, so many years before. She was in her late fifties or early sixties but looked to be in her early forties, at the most. Her short spiky hair gave her face character, and her take-no-crap attitude was apparent from miles away. I felt like I could do anything while in her presence. In particular, I was able to speak candidly and honestly without fear. Trevor was also featured heavily in the documentary, which somehow made me feel as though everything had come full circle. Here I was, back in New York, hanging out with amazing people and sharing the journey with my good friend from Canada. I felt as though the emptiness I'd carried with me for so many years was being filled. Being around such passion and dedication left me dizzy with happiness.

I was the executive director of the Long Island Maritime Museum, and there was no question—I loved my job. My office overlooked Long Island's Great South Bay, for heaven's sake! Sure, it didn't have heat or air conditioning and it smelled like feet, but it was my tiny slice of heaven.

But after my part in the documentary was finished, I started to lose my passion for my work. I'd been so thrilled initially, yet as I became more

involved in rape kit reform, my excitement about the museum began to
fade as it was overshadowed by what I'd started to recognize as my calling.
Besides that, my brain was not being very nice to me, and I found myself
again falling into some old bad habits. I'd done so much talking about my
rape, both in court and on camera, but I didn't have anyone to really talk
to, someone to help me process this new experience of openness and the
attention I was receiving. Soon my coworkers began to notice my lacklus-
ter efforts, and tensions began to build. I just didn't have the energy to take
on any more fights, so I gave the museum board one month's notice without even thinking about what I was going to do next. I knew I wanted to
use my story to help others, I just didn't know how I was going to do that
yet. Melissa Mourges and her cold-case-unit soul mate, Martha Bashford
(chief of New York County's Special Victims Division at the time of this
writing), had always left the door wide open for me. After working side by
side for so many years, they're more like family than colleagues—besides
spending most days together at work, they go on vacations together, attend
their children's graduations, and are there for each other through both success and failure. I'm sort of a fangirl around them, and I trip over myself a
little. I do, however, feel comfortable asking for their opinions, and I knew
they might be able to help me figure things out.

If you go by what's on TV, you'd expect law offices to be populated
by fancy people in designer suits and four-inch heels, seated behind
big mahogany desks in expensive leather chairs, the air perfumed by
cigars and whiskey. In reality, Melissa and Martha's office was located
in a big, old, crumbling building, and their functional assembly-line
desks were hidden behind columns of cardboard boxes stacked floor to
ceiling, with just enough space tunneled out for them to see each other
across the room. Two nondescript chairs occupied the space in front
of Melissa's desk, which I'm sure were cleared of boxes a few minutes
before, in anticipation of my arrival. As I took a seat, I wondered where
they'd stored those boxes and how in the world they'd managed to find
my file among the thousands of others.

"I want to start my own nonprofit and somehow help others," I blurted out.

Martha and Melissa exchanged glances (I swear, they have this weird telepathy thing from working together for so long). Martha said, "We were hoping you'd say something like that."

"Actually, Natasha, we don't know how many untested rape kits there are across the country. Maybe that's something you could work on," Melissa added.

Back at home I did some research. How many of these kits were just sitting on a shelf somewhere? The scariest answer was no answer: that number is unknown, but it's estimated to be in the hundreds of thousands. Think about that for a second. *Hundreds of thousands* of rape kits, sealed and untested, across the nation. Hundreds of thousands of stories and God knows how many tears. There could be another Victor Perfect Rondon in one of those kits. Another Natasha.

There was no other option. It was time to get those kits tested. I decided that I would be their champion. I would see that they'd all get done, just like they had in New York.

My good friend and coworker Melissa Parrott helped me start the journey. I knew Melissa was someone who could get things done—she and I had undertaken the daunting process of getting the paperwork in order for a wildlife-centered summer camp called Barrens to Bay. Now, time was of the essence—the documentary was coming out in June of 2011, just three short months away. We visited her friend, a lawyer by the name of Mark Murray. He offered to start the paperwork, ushering in the birth of Natasha's Justice Project.

My friend Megan Heckman left her job and joined me in the early days of Natasha's Justice Project. I maxed out all my credit cards to pay her a tiny salary. I was sure that once people found out there was a backlog, there would be outrage! Followed by a torrent of check writing and grant giving and fundraising. People would march in the streets and demand that each and every one of those tests get tested, and now. We'd be ready for them.

Unfortunately, that's not exactly what happened.

To educate myself on the current work being done in the field, I met with people from the Joyful Heart Foundation and RAINN. It was important that we worked together, side by side, without replicating one another's efforts. The only way to get this done would be as a team.

HBO flew me out to Los Angeles for the documentary's premiere. It was really exciting. I spent time with my cousin and his daughters and did a bunch of interviews with all the major news networks. There I was, just this regular person, having to be natural on camera while at the same time navigating the interviewers' agendas, stating my mission, and appealing to viewers. Somehow, even though I had a plan going in, for all those times I talked about the backlog, I didn't mention Natasha's Justice Project, much to the dismay of Mark, Melissa, and Megan back at home. Not once.

HBO had a crew of publicists working with me when the film launched. I learned what colors looked best on me on television and how to get messages across in the very short time that was allotted. I learned that I hated how my eyebrows arched when I was serious and that my curly hair was cute only when no one was there to see it. If there was a camera nearby, my hair instantly frizzed up into an absolute mess. But the HBO publicists were always on hand to tell me my hair looked great! And I was fantastic! And I was just so pretty! It made me very uncomfortable, all the compliments. I preferred harder truths—ones that aligned with my own opinion of myself—like those my mom would give me.

"Natasha, you are beautiful but, I'm sorry, your hair was a mess. But Natasha, what you said was very sincere. Your words are much more important," she'd say. Of course, she was absolutely right—the message is what matters.

It was easy to be optimistic at first. After *Sex Crimes Unit* came out, a flood of survivors reached out to me to express solidarity and compassion. I had never met so many other survivors before, and suddenly I felt as though I was marching along with an army, that I was no longer alone. I learned a lot those first few months, mostly from other survivors.

What I found most surprising, and in retrospect, perhaps shouldn't have, was how open these men and women were in sharing their stories with me. With all the trust they were placing in me, I felt comfortable sharing my story with them as well. What began to become abundantly clear was how very different the experience was for each of us in the aftermath of the assault. The details of the assault itself didn't matter as much as how we were treated afterward by friends, family, and law enforcement. I learned that too many survivors had to beg and plead to be believed. Often, they had to call attention to their assaults through the media in order to get their kits tested. We all shared a common trauma, but the re-traumatization that occurred after the fact was where we often differed.

I drew strength from the men and women I was meeting. We'd swap stories and, most importantly, we would laugh at ourselves. I had spent so many years berating myself, and it was nice to have a chuckle over the strange or self-defeating things I'd done in order to cope. We'd also share the more helpful coping tools we'd learned along the way. From these brave and kind people, I was learning more than I could possibly wrap my brain around.

I had been calling the issue of untested rape kits the "backlog" for months, only to learn that while there is a rape kit backlog, the untested kits sitting untouched in law enforcement storage facilities are not technically backlogged. The National Institute of Justice defines a backlogged kit as one that has not been tested thirty days after it was submitted to the laboratory.[17] Meaning that all kits that have not yet taken this preliminary journey to a laboratory aren't even considered "backlogged."

---

17. Mark Nelson, "Making Sense of DNA Backlogs—Myths vs. Reality," *NIJ Journal,* no. 266 (2010). https://www.nij.gov/journals/266/pages/backlogs.aspx.

Thanks to the amazing Debbie Smith and her husband, Rob, there is, in fact, money allocated for processing these kits:

> "The Debbie Smith Act of 2004 (42 U.S.C. 13701) provides United States federal government grants to eligible states and units of local government to conduct DNA analyses of backlogged DNA samples collected from victims of crimes and criminal offenders. The Act expands the Combined DNA Index System (CODIS) and provides legal assistance to survivors of dating violence. Named after sexual assault survivor Debbie Smith, the Act was passed by the 108th Congress as part of larger legislation, the Justice for All Act of 2004 (P.L. 108-405), and signed into law by President George W. Bush on October 30, 2004.[18]"

Debbie and Rob both fought tirelessly for this bill, after her rape kit experienced the same neglect mine did following her rape in 1989. (The DNA of the attacker, who was already serving time, was identified in 1995. He was sentenced to multiple life sentences in prison.)[19] Now, as a grandmother, she continues the fight—for many of us, there is always a fear that the money will be taken away and put toward something else.

After I found this out, I called my survivor friends—we jokingly call ourselves "survivors of the backlog"—and asked them if their kits were backlogged under the technical term. All twenty of them gave me the same answer: No. None of our kits had ever made it to a lab, which

---

18. Debbie Smith Act of 2004, Pub. L. 108-405, 118 Stat. 2260 (2004).

19. Kathryn M. Turman, *Understanding DNA Evidence: A Guide for Victim Service Providers—Case Studies: The Power of a DNA Match*, accessed July 6, 2017, https://ojp.gov/ovc/publications/bulletins/dna_4_2001/dna11_4_01.html.

meant that the Debbie Smith Act wouldn't cover them. Some of my friends didn't even know where their kits were. I also knew survivors who'd been raped by someone they knew, and they'd been told flat out by the police that their kit would never be tested. Worst of all, others had undergone the rape kit exam but were still trying to convince the police that they were telling the truth in the first place, that a crime had been committed. The problem was bigger than I had imagined.

I was fortunate to have several friends I could bounce ideas off of, Kim Lembo in particular. Kim is a petite firecracker, a veritable bundle of energy whom it's impossible to sit still around. She used to work in Silicon Valley and has maintained an amazing network of techie friends. Her ability to motivate and stay positive is almost unrivaled—and so we put our heads together to do some serious fundraising for the project.

First we spent hours scouring the Internet for details on rape and assault laws and legislation. We met with prosecutors and technicians to gain a better understanding of the issues at hand and to hear ideas about how to solve them from those in the field. The more we learned, the more bewildered and, yes, angry I became.

One in six women is sexually assaulted in the United States.[20] That is 16 percent of all women. Men, of course, are sexually assaulted as well, but, unfortunately, those statistics are difficult to determine because sex crimes against men are so underreported.

You would think that a crime that occurs so very often would get taken seriously. Sadly, it isn't. And soon Kim and I discovered that unprocessed rape kits were just the tip of a very deep iceberg.

Part of the problem—or, perhaps, the main problem—was that people simply did not want to discuss the issue with us, or at all. Those

20. "Victims of Sexual Violence: Statistics," RAINN, accessed July 27, 2017, https://www.rainn.org/statistics/victims-sexual-violence.

reporters who were willing to propose the subject as worthy of coverage to their producers were shot down, told in no uncertain terms that rape and rape victims were likely lying. Prosecutors said they simply didn't have the manpower to prosecute the number of people who would end up being charged with sexual assault if all the kits were tested. Rape victims told us they weren't going to press the issue because they were afraid. It was beginning to feel as though rape was considered, if anything, a hassle, not a crime.

Every time I was about to give up—and there were plenty of times, after someone dismissed my cause or told me not to waste my time, when I felt my resolve start to flag—I would meet a survivor, who'd approach me with tears in her eyes. Sometimes that was the moment when she would share her experience for the very first time. That trust and faith in me re-lit my fire—no one was giving up on me, and so I wasn't about to give up on them, either.

I was determined to get Natasha's Justice Project off the ground, come what may. But I was horrible at asking for money. Though I was able to get meetings with potential donors, I always felt guilty asking for support. At the same time, I was making promises to survivors, and I felt guilty for not being able to keep them.

On top of that, to keep things going I had been paying out of pocket, and I was running out of room on my credit cards. I borrowed money from my mother just so that I could buy an eighty-eight-cent package of precooked hot dogs and a one-dollar loaf of bread from the Aldi around the corner. Kim would fly me out to San Francisco on her dime so we could brainstorm. I didn't want anyone to know how desperate things had become, and I didn't have the heart to tell her that I didn't have enough money to pay my electric bill. I felt compelled to continue, even as I dug myself into a hole. I would—*I had to*—find a way somehow.

In February of 2012 I woke up shivering. Zoë had curled herself into a tight ball next to me beneath the comforter, and I could feel her little body trembling, too. I remembered that unpaid bill, followed by a warning and another warning from the electric company. Finally, my power had been shut off.

I was particularly frustrated because I knew that in two days we'd be meeting with a potential donor, who seemed to be very interested in the issue. How would I be able to convince her to give me a big chunk of money if I hadn't even been able to raise enough money to pay my utility bills?

I called Mark Murray, the lawyer who'd submitted the paperwork for Natasha's Justice Project (NJP) pro bono. He took me out for drinks at our favorite rustic Italian restaurant, La Tavola, where we'd gotten to know the friendly staff and manager. Mark is something of a wine expert, and he always picks a fabulous bottle off the menu. Over a glass of Burgundy, I shared the whole story with him: how the meetings went nowhere, how I'd found so many people who wanted to help but needed direction, and how hard it was to explain the issue of unprocessed rape kits to people. There were just so many layers to it, and so many emotions and silenced voices, that I had been unable to come up with that essential elevator speech. Almost as a side note I told him that my house was without power, and I had an interview with CBS the next day.

Mark immediately invited Zoë and me into his home. We joined his family for dinner, and in the company of his three lovely daughters—who have since become like sisters to me—I forgot my troubles for a while.

"I'll be going with you to these meetings from now on," he said at the end of the night.

"Thank you," I replied, beyond grateful.

From that moment on, Mark Murray was NJP's official closer. It became clear to us both that asking for money was just not my thing. He was good at it, very good. At the first meeting, we received a donation for $25,000, and another $25,000 shortly thereafter. I still didn't feel comfortable drawing a paycheck, but at least I could be reimbursed for my travel expenses and some of Megan's salary. It was enough to have my lights turned back on. I sold my car and breathed a sigh of relief—we'd be OK for a little while longer.

I wish that was the end of that part of the story, and that from there it was smooth sailing. Turns out it's much easier to raise money for a tech start-up than it is for a project to get rape kits processed, and Natasha's Justice Project has struggled financially ever since. Still, it amazes me how every time I am just about to give up, something propels me to go back in the ring for another round. My power has been turned off three times in total, and I have zero credit to my name. But what we have managed to accomplish is nothing short of miraculous.

I was on the news quite a bit from 2012 to 2015, and I still get invitations from time to time. Unfortunately, news cycles change frequently, and the topic of sexual assault is often sidelined for celebrity gossip and political intrigue, especially these days when every half hour a news bulletin breaks. This project, meanwhile, is a slow slog and not always exciting, and it's difficult for reporters to pitch to their producers. There is a fear that we will turn off viewers, that they can handle a police shooting or a corruption scandal but not thousands of rape victims seeking justice through the clogged channels of due process. Frankly, I don't think we give people enough credit, and bringing this topic to light is a big part of the battle. There are so many dedicated reporters out there who continue to push for the green light to cover this issue. And there are plenty of people in the media who report on this topic no matter what kind of pushback they get—it means that much to them. Most of the folks I've met in this line of work go into it for altruistic reasons and want to serve the public thirst for knowledge. I think that is why they and I get along so well. We share a mission—to spread the word in a way that will galvanize the masses.

6.

SHAKING OFF THE DUST

"Every problem has a solution."
—Mom

As the years tick by, I find myself reflecting upon Natasha's Justice Project's achievements.

My team and I have worked tirelessly to create an organization that can efficiently expose and eliminate the issue of untested rape kits across the United States. Many of my fellow backlog survivors and I have testified before Congress and have undergone multiple interviews with the media. We get up there and share our stories with the world in an attempt to make a difference. I can tell you honestly that none of us are particularly fond of the spotlight, nor have any of us gotten rich from this venture. But we are doing the best we can, because we are compelled to. Because we must.

Having the opportunity to meet with other survivors has been one of the greatest blessings of my life. It's so helpful to have someone you can brainstorm with, process with, vent to. It's harder to throw in the towel when you know someone is just a phone call away, willing to pick you up when you're down.

It has also become clear to me that we are all survivors of something or another. It's amazing how there are always ways to relate, no matter how different we may seem at first glance. I have found such strength in hearing from others who have been able to come out of a bad situation and find peace on the other end. Pete Bergen and his lovely wife, Brooke, are an example of this—they reached out to me on social media after hearing my story in *Sex Crimes Unit*. Pete and Brooke know everyone in Washington, D.C., and they offered to throw a fundraiser for Natasha's Justice Project. Stand Up for Natasha's Justice Project, a stand-up comedy fundraiser, is an ongoing yearly event in the D.C. area, and of the four put on so far, all have sold out. Pete is one of the funniest human beings I know, and his openness about his addiction and recovery serves as an inspiration. I learned from Pete that it doesn't have to be dark all the time. Laughter has an amazing way of putting people at ease and making a very scary thing a lot easier to face. Every show is followed with a question-and-answer session. One of the questions is the same every time: Why isn't anyone doing anything about this problem?

In 2012, my posttraumatic stress disorder had taken hold once again. Not that it ever goes away, but over the years, I had learned to accept my ups and downs, to plow ahead as best I could. Often, I'd have a drink when I felt the darkness closing in on me. I could go for weeks managing in this way, feeling not great but good enough, or functional at least. Then I'd get to a bridge.

No, I'm not talking about some metaphorical bridge. I mean a real steel or concrete bridge, the kind you drive or walk or bike across to get to the other side. Apparently, fear of bridges—or gephyrophobia, in scientific terms—is not uncommon, although an exact number of people who suffer from it is hard to determine. Like many phobias, it stems from an irrational fear, which is usually a symptom of some deeper fear. For me, it started with being a little uncomfortable when I knew I'd be taking a ride over a long bridge, but I was able to shrug it off and take that ride. As the fear escalated, I tried to avoid going to places that required a large bridge crossing as part of the journey. Finally, I found myself having nightmares about driving over the largest bridge ever. All the dreams are virtually the same: I'm driving down the road, and all of a sudden, a huge bridge looms up ahead. It's impossibly long and high, and I take one look and know that there is no way I will make it across. I decide that I'll take the next exit instead. Soon it becomes clear that there is no exit, and it's too late to turn back—I've reached the point of no return, and I have no choice but to cross the bridge. I get halfway up the incline and freeze. I stop the car. All the drivers around me begin honking their horns and screaming at me. I decide to ditch my car and get out to walk. Standing there makes me dizzy, so on hands and knees, I crawl the rest of the way, feeling the whole time like I'm about to go over the edge. I always wake up before I make it across.

Along with that recurring nightmare, during the day I was increasingly experiencing moments of disconnection. Sometimes, I'd be in a busy public place and suddenly feel that if I did not hold on to something, I would become unmoored and zip around like a balloon filled with helium. At busy restaurants, I'd have to brace myself against the table in an attempt to remain grounded. Talk about awkward—try explaining that to your dining companions, who are simply trying to enjoy a nice meal. Not that I understood it enough to explain it. Even though I knew in my logical mind that the odds of dying on bridges were probably lower than the odds of dying in the car ride itself and that flying away was a physical impossibility, my animal brain and body weren't getting the message.

One day, I was hanging out with a group of survivors, and we began to discuss the silly things we find ourselves doing to cope. I decided to disclose my strange behavior, hoping they would laugh. To my surprise, they all just nodded their heads and said "Mmmhmm" and "Oh, yeah, that happens to me all the time." Apparently, the sensation of leaving your body is not uncommon among survivors of trauma. It makes sense—for most of us, we had to dissociate during the event or events that initially traumatized us as a way to survive. Afterward, the only way to leave the scene of the crime is to leave our bodies. In order to do the important work of Natasha's Justice Project, I was frequently sharing my story, and in order to guard against being overwhelmed by the painful memories of that experience, I would emotionally detach myself from the words I was speaking. Simply put, if I were to get emotional every time I shared my story, I would be an absolute mess. However, creating that distance had taken its toll and was expressing itself in inappropriate and unhelpful ways.

I decided it was time to take an honest inventory of myself. I was completely broke, I was not making the best choices, I was miserable. It's hard for me to admit this, but I'd begun to doubt humanity as a whole—people just *didn't care*. So many promises had been broken—even those journalists with genuine enthusiasm for the project wouldn't follow up after the first interview. The media needed to hold police departments accountable by reporting on how many rape kits had been discovered and, later, whether or not they'd actually been tested and entered into a database. The audience needed to know that this was an ongoing process, and to receive an update about our progress and where we needed more help. Those reporting one-offs made me sad. On top of that, a bunch of donations had fallen through. I'd met billionaires—that's *billionaires*, with a *B*—who had flown me out, treated me to some of the fanciest dinners I'd ever had, shown me around their lavish homes, and said, "Oh, well, we'll see what we can do," and then vanished. Or they'd have their assistant call me with their credit card, then donate less than what they'd spent on the bottle of wine at dinner. That hurt so very badly.

In 2013, I stepped away from the work. (I would soon learn, however, that the work would not step away from me.) I felt it wasn't fair to be anything less than my very best if I was going to represent our movement.

The first hurdle I ran into was the fact that I didn't understand or believe that I had PTSD. I'd seen firsthand that when veterans return from war they often struggle with their emotions. But how could my experience possibly compare to what they have been through?

To avoid having to acknowledge my stress or my terror, I self-medicated with alcohol or cough medicine. I beat myself up over not being like everyone else. I felt guilty that I couldn't do things the way others did, that I couldn't just breeze through life. For me, everything was a challenge. I worked hard to get out of bed, and I worked hard to go to sleep. Most nights I'd wake up from a nightmare and check the house for intruders with a baseball bat in hand. I would turn on every light one by one and turn up the TV to full volume. When I lived alone, I would pretend to have conversations with someone else so that an intruder wouldn't know that I was by myself.

I couldn't bear to be without something to do. My mind constantly needed to be active so that it wouldn't slip into dark thoughts and memories. Every part of my body had to be active in order for me to stay distracted. I couldn't do just one activity—if I were watching TV, I was also reading a book and eating popcorn at the same time. At the same time, mundane tasks like taking a shower or doing the dishes were very difficult for me to accomplish.

Another issue that I frankly thought was unrelated was my inability to find things where I had left them. Probably the most common trigger for panic mode was misplacing my car keys. For whatever reason, they never seemed to be where I remembered leaving them. But keys were far from the only thing that would disappear into my brain fog. Virtually anything I put down would be lost to me. Anyone who knows me can vouch for this—spend a day with me and you'd see me shuffling through my purse in a panic, looking for something or another. It's just what I do.

It wasn't until I was with a group of survivors that I realized all of these "quirks" were related to my trauma. The therapist leading the group said that when you're a survivor or a victim of trauma, your brain is constantly on high alert and unable to recall where you placed your keys because it's too busy checking your surroundings to make sure you're safe. This is an old-school survival mechanism: In a small community of hunters and gatherers, it was essential to be hypervigilant. Light sleepers would hear the lion before it pounced, while their more relaxed counterparts would wake up to a set of teeth on their throats. Today, there's usually no reason for this primitive switch to be turned on. For me, and others who've experienced trauma, it's like the switch is always turned on, and turning it off can be difficult or even impossible. And mundane but necessary everyday processes, like remembering where I left my purse or where I put down my soda, get disrupted.

I was raped in 1993 and finally accepted my PTSD in 2013—twenty years later.

I wish I had some sort of miracle cure to offer up. Lord knows I've spent plenty of time looking for one.

I met with psychiatrist Dr. Greene, who specialized in utilizing medication for PTSD. He worked mostly with veterans, and he assured me that many of our issues were similar and suggested I try Zoloft. In 2013, Zoloft was one of the only medications approved by the FDA for the treatment of PTSD. Initially, I was worried about how the medication might make me feel.

"You won't be a zombie," Dr. Greene assured me.

After six weeks of Zoloft treatment, I didn't really notice any difference. Until the day I was watching reruns of *Friends* on TV and found myself laughing out loud. I really didn't think anything of it until that started to happen on a regular basis. I was LOLing!

The second thing I noticed was that I now had a beat, so to speak, before I reacted. In the past, if something stressed me out, I would react impulsively without having a chance to think it through. Somehow,

Zoloft allowed me to pause long enough to analyze the situation before responding. That is not to say that I didn't freak out on occasion; it just meant that I had more power to *decide* whether or not to let loose.

Less freaking out meant more time to meditate, which I also found helpful. Granted, I don't meditate nearly as much as I'd like to, but it's a tool in my arsenal that I can use as needed. It doesn't so much make my problematic thoughts go away as it makes me take a second to reflect and accept my surroundings.

I also began playing video games again. Massively multiplayer online role-playing games with complex structures and plots, like Final Fantasy XIV, seem to work best for me. How could I think about terrible things while I was beating up dragons and flying through the air on griffins? In Final Fantasy Online, I found a community of individuals who were as flawed and introspective as I am. That was very comforting.

Through my gamer community and my survivor community, I came to realize that even when people appear to be going through life with ease, that's not always the case. We all wear masks. We are all struggling through something, no matter how confident we may seem from the outside. I can attribute my own progress with openness to this realization—the more open I am with others, the more open others are with me. Often, I'd find out that people who I assumed were just breezing through life were actually going through some really hard challenges. To learn that we are all beautifully flawed has been quite enlightening. I have—and will probably always have—bad days. The difference now is that I know that things will eventually turn around because I am not alone. This, too, has allowed me to be better at accepting myself, flaws and all. It is something I work on daily.

Perhaps my most unique treatment has been the practice of lucid dreaming. This has been extremely helpful for dealing with my nightmares. While I cannot do it consistently, I have gotten better over time. The idea is that you can sort of wake up in the middle of the dream, and once you "wake up," you can control the situation around you. You can do anything you like! You can fly!

In the past, when I would have a nightmare, I would be at the mercy of whatever I was facing in the dream. Now, during the day, I check my surroundings to make sure everything is firmly grounded in reality. I try to do the same when I'm dreaming, so if something seems "off" or out of place, that's my cue to take control. Although it doesn't work every night, I'm no longer so scared to go to sleep. And my boyfriend, Scott, is rarely roused awake by my nighttime screams.

After accepting myself, the next most important thing is that I make sure that the people around me are aware of my challenges and accept me for who I am. I tell them what I need, and I tell them when I'm upset. It's taken me a long time to figure that out and be OK with it.

Do what you will with this information—none of it is meant to be advice. We are not all the same, and what I do may not be a good method for everyone. My choices and my choice of treatment may even be dangerous for someone else.

I've asked other survivors what they do to control their PTSD, and they've given me lots of different answers. For some people, medication was a good start. Others, not so much. Most of us do agree that it's not about controlling or getting rid of our PTSD, it's about coping. And that's OK.

One thing I realized during my self-imposed break was that I and my fellow survivors had more to offer than what we were giving. We'd shared our stories over a variety of media, and our pictures graced newspapers across the country. But more and more, we felt like we were being used as props. Several survivors had told me stories of how they'd been passed over for victims who were more "raw," those who would meet the expectation of what a victim is supposed to look like, or guarantee that they'd tell their stories through ratings-boosting tears. We were often invited to join case studies and focus groups, held across the country by various organizations. During these meetings, we were asked for our opinion on a range of things. What did we think were the best practices for notifying a victim whose kit has not been tested for years? Should it be a phone call? An e-mail? A visit in person? They loved to use hypotheticals—for example, what if a woman had not told her husband that she'd been raped, then later found out that she'd gotten pregnant by her rapist and decided to keep the baby? How should this woman be told that her rape kit had been tested?

I'm not sure my input was particularly helpful, since I really could only claim to know what it was I would want. And I suspected that they'd already come up with a one-size-fits-all conclusion, and that they used us just so they could say that they'd incorporated survivor input. Our suggestions wouldn't actually be implemented; this wasn't a true collaboration, however good the intentions of these organizations were. We were beginning to feel as if it were all for show or that we were just a bunch of lab rats, and that people were taking advantage of our pain.

If we wanted to be thought of as more than just the sum of our traumatic stories, we had to make certain we were doing more than just retelling them. It wasn't easy to get a real seat at the table with the academics, law professors, and policy makers we met with regularly. While they were extremely kind and thoughtful, I don't believe they quite considered us colleagues. That just didn't seem fair to me. Any successful movement has to include the people most affected by the issue, right? Like a roomful of male politicians discussing women's healthcare, when it came to the serious decisions regarding policy or grants, no one was asking for our input.

Like many of my fellow survivors, I started to travel the country to urge legislators to adopt measures to get rape kits off the shelves and into the laboratories. Some folks didn't know that the labs could apply for funding through Debbie Smith's grants, and so I set about spreading the word. It was hard work. Many legislators were simple unaware of the issue to begin with, and sometimes it was easier to convince them to introduce legislation that would force jurisdictions to count how many unprocessed kits were in their inventory, rather than try to get them to inventory *and* test *and* catalogue. And then there was the matter of convincing them that this was not like spending money on cleaning out their closets—this was about public safety.

As I became more involved in this aspect of the work, more policy makers began to contact me to ask for collaboration on various pieces of legislation. See the Appendices for examples. I started testifying before the House and Senate on a regular basis. While I had visited D.C. in the past, the city suddenly took on a new meaning for me. I, a child of immigrants, was participating in lawmaking, helping lawmakers make the country a safer place. The buildings I now had access to were full of history, of the mistakes we've made and the changes we've fought so hard for. Seeing the inner workings of our democracy allowed me to better understand what it means to be an elected official and to see that even though such people often get a bad rap, everyone I met truly wanted to do the right thing.

Senator Dick Black, a Republican who served in Virginia's House of Delegates from 1998 to 2006 and was elected to the state senate in 2011, called me out of the blue one day to say he had read a brochure about Natasha's Justice Project and now wanted to pass legislation to count unprocessed rape kits.

Some of my colleagues were taken aback when I mentioned this unexpected conversation—they were not fans of Senator Black, who has "set the high-water mark" for antichoice legislation and has received an A grade from the National Rifle Association for his originalist interpretation of the Second Amendment. Oddly enough, considering his interest in the Natasha's Justice Project, he'd been opposed to making spousal rape a crime. His record on women's rights wasn't good: he'd called emergency contraception "baby pesticide," had compared *Roe v. Wade* to the Holocaust, had voted for the bill that would require women seeking abortions to have transvaginal ultrasounds, and had sent pink plastic fetuses to senators. He'd even claimed that gay-straight alliances promoted sex and led to the spread of AIDS. Despite their— and my—misgivings, I found my conversations with the senator to be quite enlightening and productive. He understood the issue and was really passionate about rape kit reform.

Senator Black called and texted me throughout the process. No, not a staffer—*he* stayed in touch on a regular basis to ask questions, give me updates, ask if I'd seen a pertinent article in the newspaper.

When Senate Bill 658[21] was ready to be signed by the governor of Virginia in 2016, Senator Black invited me to the press conference. The room was filled with members of the media from across the state and Washington, D.C., and I appreciated being invited to this important event. I stood in the crowd, thrilled that Virginia had passed the legislation. When it was Senator Black's turn at the podium, he did something that changed the way I viewed public officials. Rather than taking the recognition for himself, he called me forward. I didn't write the bill, but he gave all the credit to me. I was shocked.

After the conference, a woman from the National Organization for Women and a woman from a Virginia-based advocacy group approached the senator to talk about some of his stances on women's rights. He was open to the conversation, but he did something strange, which to this day I'm not sure he was conscious of. We were standing at one of those conference snack tables, and he grabbed two oranges and a banana and held them in a . . . certain way. *Oh my gosh, this man is a walking, talking Freudian slip!!* I couldn't help but think. *But I'm*

---

21. Physical evidence recovery kits; local and state law-enforcement agencies shall report an inventory, Va. S.B. 658 (2014).

probably the only one who noticed. At this point, I felt a little bit protective of him.

"We may not agree on some things," I said, "but at the end of the day, we are all just doing what we believe in our hearts is right."

Now, I'm not naive, and I know that sometimes politicians are motivated by more than just altruism. But I also know that we have to take our allies where we find them, and Senator Black has been invaluable to this cause. In 2015, Senator Black went on to pass Senate Bill 712,[22] designed to protect women from sexual assault on college campuses and to hold institutions accountable for reporting cases to law enforcement.

After he walked away, one of the women said, "Did you see the 'two tangerine banana dick' thing?"

In 2014, I was invited to serve on the Rape Kit Action Project (RKAP), a national coalition to develop laws and best practices for rape kits. It was humbling for me to sit alongside experts from RAINN, the National Center for Victims of Crime, and the Joyful Heart Foundation. Finally I felt as though I was being recognized as more than just my story, being taken seriously as a colleague and friend.

When I first joined the RKAP, I was starstruck. Ilse Knecht, the director of policy and advocacy for the Joyful Heart Foundation, had been conducting webinars across the country, encouraging law enforcement to take a better look at the evidence and understand the value of testing all kits. She has firmly established herself as one of the nation's leaders on sexual assault and trauma education and advocacy. Ilse is one of the most mission-oriented people I know, and she's not afraid to share her opinion on anything. She is also funny as hell. You have to hold on to your sense of humor with a tight grip in this line of work.

---

22. Higher education; handling of sexual assault cases. Va. S.B. 712 (2015).

People often assume we shared hotel rooms to cut costs, but that's actually not the case. We frequently shared hotel rooms so that we could stay up all night and swap stories, like sisters would.

Rebecca O'Connor is the Rape, Abuse and Incest National Network's vice president of public policy. A former lawyer, Becca joined RAINN to use her expertise for making sure bills are passed. A mother of twins, she never stops moving, not even for a second. She's the kind of person who remembers everyone's birthday, and she's the first person to ask you how you are feeling if she hears you've been under the weather. Becca would give you her last penny if you needed it.

While I see rape kit reform legislation as beneficial no matter what (it gets people talking about the issue), some laws are better than others. Like all things government, this is a very complicated process—it took me a while to understand how the whole thing works. Here is how I explain it in my own way:

The Tenth Amendment to our United States Constitution states that "the powers not delegated to the United States by the Constitution, nor prohibited by it to the States, are reserved to the States respectively, or to the people."[23]

This is what people are talking about when they say "states' rights." What this means is that the federal government cannot force a state to abide by a law the federal government creates. The federal government can create guidelines or make suggestions and even hold back federal funding if states choose not to participate, but that's about it. It's for this reason that rape kit reform needs to be addressed on a state-by-state basis. In the end, it's up to every state to develop rules around how rape kits are processed.

The best-case scenario for the elimination of rape kit backlog would require states to adopt three important laws, in this order:

---

23. U.S. Const. amend. X.

1. Count all rape kits that are as yet untested.
2. Create a timeline for completion of testing.
3. Create a tracking system to ensure that all rape kits are tested and the results entered into a national database going forward.

If these three simple laws are put into place in every state across the nation, we'll be in good shape. The first challenge is to find a lawmaker willing to write the bill and stand behind it until it becomes law. Ideally, there will be two lawmakers, or sponsors, per state, each from a different side of the aisle.

Usually, people are on board in theory, but actually making these three basic public safety measures a reality comes down to money, or lack thereof. It's not really a matter of finding money as much as it is convincing officials to spend money on this particular issue. This has never made sense to me. Think of how much money the nation would have been saved if my kit had been tested sooner. Although each rape kit costs between $1,000 and $1,500 to process,[24] that's a bargain compared to what Victor Rondon and his one-man crime spree cost taxpayers. Not to mention what it cost me and his other victims. According to RAINN, approximately $12.9 billion a year would have been saved in terms of medical costs, lost wages, and other tangible harms to victims and society caused by serial offenders. So if the fact that it's the right thing to do isn't persuasive enough, just take a look at the bottom line.

You would think that that first step—counting unprocessed rape kits—would be easy and relatively inexpensive. Surely there is a database somewhere with all that information, and, after a few keystrokes, the numbers pop up. This couldn't be further from the reality. There are

---

24. "Why the Backlog Exists," End the Backlog, accessed July 27, 2017, http://www.endthebacklog.org/backlog/why-backlog-exists.

jurisdictions across the country that do not even have a computer, let alone the software required. Plus there's little or no protocol for where rape kits should go from the hospital.

In Texas, for example, over 20,000 unprocessed kits were discovered.[25] Detroit's backlog numbered around 11,000,[26] and Wayne County Prosecutor Kym Worthy fought tooth and nail for funding. In Memphis in 2013, the police department found over 12,000 unprocessed kits,[27] with advocates estimating that the number was actually much larger. It took city officials and advocates from the Joyful Heart Foundation years to count them—the kits were scattered all over the place. Some kits were in police storage, while others were found at the University of Tennessee College of Medicine. Even worse, some kits had not even left the hospital. Because of this, a class action lawsuit has been brought against the city of Memphis on behalf of the victims. This highlights a split within the survivor community: We're all angry about this negligence, and rightfully so. Our approach to resolving it is where the divide becomes evident—for some, anger at and distrust and fear of the police and government has created an inability or unwillingness to partner with them to solve the problem. It can be difficult for those police or elected officials who want to make amends for the mistakes of their predecessors and yet are met with resistance from those they're trying to help. Every now and then, as someone who has worked and continues to work with anyone who is interested, I've been on the receiving end of this anger, even being called a "government mule." And yet, I can feel nothing but compassion for my fellow survivors who have been greatly injured by those who were responsible for protecting

25. https://judiciary.house.gov/_files/hearings/printers/111th/111-115_56523.PDF
26. Rosie Swash, "Kym Worthy and the fight to investigate Detroit's 11,000 forgotten rapes," The Guardian, August 26, 2013.
27. "Memphis police: 12,000 backlogged rape kits tested, suspects ID'd," Chicago Tribune, March 10, 2015.

them. This damage cannot be undone. I wish not just that all victims had been treated with respect after the crime, but that none of us had been victimized to begin with.

I am always thrilled to meet officials who truly believe in what we are doing. My good friend and superhero, Nancy O'Malley, district attorney of Alameda, California, has been trying to get attention on this issue since the late 1980s—she's been fundamental to rape kit reform and truly deserves more credit. In 2012, I'd been calling jurisdictions around the country to see whether they had any untested kits. Nine times out of ten they'd hang up on me. But not Nancy. After seeing *Sex Crimes Unit* she was determined to get her city's untested rape kits counted and processed. And she did, raising the funds and, with Deputy District Attorneys Jason Chin and Annie Saadi, going to each hospital in the county to find out how many victims had undergone the rape kit exam. After they established that number, they went to each police station and asked where each and every kit was. They quickly uncovered over 2,000 sexual assault evidence kits that had never been tested.[28]

No one knows the exact numbers, but it is estimated that nationwide there are hundreds of thousands of rape kits that have been shelved for decades. This information is alarming. But I'd much rather know the size and weight of the problem than not. Knowing is half—well, in this case, one-third—of the battle.

Once you find out just how many kits have been collecting dust, you must put a time frame on testing them and then uploading the results to a shared cataloguing system. In a perfect world it would take hours, but realistically, we've suggested a time frame of thirty days for the police to get the kit to the lab, and thirty days to get the kit tested and for a DNA profile to be uploaded into CODIS.

---

28. Paul T. Rosynsky, "Alameda County gets $500,000 to reduce rape kit backlog," *The Mercury News*, March 28, 2013.

I think transparency around the entire process is critical to its success. I can track my Amazon purchase every step of the way. I'm notified via text, and I know exactly where my package is at any given moment. Why can't rape kits also be tracked in a similar fashion? Victims, hospitals, law enforcement, prosecutors, and legislators should all have access to this tracking mechanism. If everyone knows where the kit is, it's less likely to get lost or abandoned. Most importantly, the victim will know precisely where the kit is in the process. I really feel this step puts teeth behind timeline legislation. Basically, if you're transparent about where in the process a kit is, you're held accountable for it. Knowing that a victim is watching will hopefully be motivating as well.

It's a lot. When you have red tape to deal with, there are all kinds of provisions you need to make. I've learned to never trust a "should"—if a bill doesn't say "must" or "shall" or "will," then it's not worth the paper it's written on. Plus, things are in a constant state of flux, and what worked well yesterday might not do its job tomorrow. For example, in 2015 the Fayetteville Police Department in North Carolina determined that 333 rape kits from unsolved assaults had been destroyed to make room for other evidence. So, once we discovered that police departments were destroying kits without the victims' knowledge or consent,[29] we had to add a provision about disposing of and destroying kits.

In 2014, with our plan laid out, we just had to start getting the money pouring in.

---

29. Ashley Fantz and Dana Ford, "Rape kits untested in Kentucky, destroyed in North Carolina," CNN, September 22, 2015, http://www.cnn.com/2015/09/21/us/kentucky-rape-kits-untested/index.html; http://www.thestate.com/news/nation-world/national/article83248387.html; https://www.theguardian.com/society/2015/nov/10/sexual-assault-rape-kit-backlog-ignored-destroyed.

7.

All of Us Everywhere

"A little birdie told me . . ."
—Mom

On April 13, 2014, the *Washington Post* editorial board wrote a piece titled "Let's Get Rape Evidence off the Shelves and Start Solving Crimes."[30]

> ALL NATASHA S. Alexenko wanted to do after she was raped at gunpoint by an unknown assailant in 1993 was take a shower. But feeling a responsibility to help police solve the crime, she submitted to an exhaustive four-hour physical exam. Never did she imagine that the rape kit—the physical

---

30. Editorial, *The Washington Post*, April 13, 2014, https://www.washington-post.com/opinions/lets-get-rape-evidence-off-the-shelves-and-start-solving-crimes/2014/04/13/3892ec52-bf5b-11e3-b574-f8748871856a_story.html?utm_term=.7b49335a2804.

evidence—would sit on a shelf in a police property room for more than nine years. Eventually the rape kit was processed and her attacker imprisoned, but hundreds of thousands of rape kits are thought to be languishing in crime storage facilities across the country.

There's a backlog because jurisdictions lack the resources or have no interest in processing the kits. That is unacceptable, Ms. Alexenko rightly says. Not only does it add to the anguish of victims, but it lets perpetrators escape accountability for their actions and perhaps attack again. Congress must give serious attention to a proposal for a new federal initiative to help localities deal with this public safety problem.

President Obama's fiscal 2015 budget proposal would for the first time allocate $35 million in dedicated funding to help local law enforcement agencies reduce the backlog in rape kits. To qualify for grants from the US Justice Department, communities would have to do more than just test the evidence; they would have to create multidisciplinary teams to investigate and prosecute cases connected to the backlog, reengaging survivors in the system and addressing the systemic failures that allowed the backlog in the first place.

The proposal, which complements existing funding for DNA testing under the Debbie Smith Act, is based on the powerful experience of police agencies who test all rape kits in their custody and not just—as is the case with many agencies—the ones for cases in which there is a suspect, or charges have been filed, or police believe the victim. When New York City implemented mandatory rape kit testing, the arrest rate for rape increased from 40 percent to 70 percent. When Detroit tested its first 1,600 kits, it found 87 serial rapists and linked its stored evidence to crimes in 21 states and the District, according to the Joyful Heart Foundation, which is advocating for solutions to the backlog.

Congress, which must appropriate the funds if the program is to become a reality, is understandably leery of new grant programs, particularly with the pressures on the federal budget. It's clear, though, that past efforts to deal with these issues have fallen short and a new approach is needed.

It's funny how a newspaper can say in a few short paragraphs what I had been trying to say for years. That fall, in November of 2014, I received a phone call from my friends at the DA's office. Cyrus Vance was soon to make an announcement about a grant program, and he wanted me there with him to do it. The next day. These were my heroes; of course I'd drop everything for them. DA Vance had a plan to put $35 million in forfeiture money toward helping other cities test their unprocessed rape kits.[31] By now, I was keenly aware of how good I had it in the hands of the New York County DA's office. New York County and New York City are nowhere near perfect. But as a whole, they have a pretty good system. No one "decides" which kits to test—they test every single rape kit that comes in. According to the FBI, they are doing something right. Nationwide, the arrest rate for rape is 22 percent. In New York, where

31. See note 4 above.

every kit is tested, the arrest rate is 74 percent, a significant success that cannot possibly be ignored.[32]

On November 12, 2014, I had the honor of standing onstage at a press conference with Prosecutor Kym Worthy from Detroit, District Attorney Cyrus R. Vance from Manhattan, and actor and activist Mariska Hargitay from *Law and Order: Special Victims Unit* and Joyful Heart Foundation. Everyone gave very moving speeches (I still get chills just thinking about them). I spoke too, and when I was finished, I made my way backstage, where Ms. Hargitay was waiting for me with a hug. For some reason, I put my head on her shoulder. Then I thought to myself, *What the hell am I doing? This woman doesn't know me!* An Associated Press photographer captured the moment forever in a photo. It turned out to be a lovely shot, and only I can tell that I'm feeling very awkward.

News about the backlog is like all news: it's hot for a second, but it becomes old news before you know it. For about a week after the conference I was inundated with calls from the media. I said yes to just about everyone, no matter how exhausted I was, because I knew that soon the phone would stop ringing. Just when I start hitting my stride, the public's attention turns to something else, and we are back fighting to get some more spotlight. Fortunately, we were about to hit grant money gold again!

On September 10, 2015, Vice President Joe Biden and DA Vance announced that the US Department of Justice would be dedicating $41 million in federal grant money to test 70,000 unprocessed rape kits nationwide. Combined with the Manhattan DA's money, that brought the grand total to nearly $80 million.[33] But Uncle Joe's money came with a lot more—it came with renewed attention toward the issue.

I remember sharing the great news with my boyfriend, Scott.

---

32. 2011 FBI report on arrest rates for sexual assault.
33. See note 5 above.

Scott and I had met in July 2012. My friend Mandy and I had just walked into the bar when a friend of his approached us and offered to buy us drinks. We followed him to the bar, where another man was casually leaning against a wall, drink in hand. In that moment, it was as though the entire room had been reduced to black and white, and he was the only thing in color. He was the most handsome man I had ever seen in my whole life. I whispered to his friend, "You're very nice, but who is he?" The friend waved Scott over.

We became a couple very quickly. He took everything in stride, stood by me and my neuroses, flakiness, and flat-out lying. I had never been loved so hard in my entire life. I had never felt so comfortable loving someone. He was what I'd always wanted and needed.

Scott is my polar opposite in many respects. Where I am a dreamer, his feet are planted firmly in reality. Because of that, he didn't quite share my enthusiasm over the $80 million grants.

"Are you going to be involved somehow?" he asked, likely knowing full well the answer was no. "You have to tell them they need you."

He was right. But, as I've mentioned, asking for things, especially when it's something specifically for me, is not my strong suit.

Besides being handsome and grounded, Scott excels at getting me to recognize my worth. He always makes certain I know how important survivors are in this dialogue. He doesn't mince words, either. We were absolutely broke. Thankfully, we had a roof over our heads—my grandmother's roof, which was now leak-free because of one of the many remodeling projects I'd undertaken over the years. The doorknobs still fell off on occasion and something always needed fixing, but it was home. Along with Piper, whom we'd adopted after Zoë lost her battle with cancer, we were happily settled. Scott, Piper, and I try to out-stubborn each other on a regular basis—it's our favorite pastime. But on this issue, I knew that Scott was not just right but bound to out-stubborn me.

DA Vance's and Uncle Joe's allocation got the ball moving in a lot of ways. Suddenly, my in-box was flooded with e-mails from lawmakers from eighteen different states across the nation, asking for help with rape kit reform. All the survivor advocates I knew were busy, running from one end of the country to the other to speak at conferences dedicated to the agenda of processing rape kits.

In 2015 I began writing legislators across the nation, urging them to take this next step to improve transparency and accountability:

> Dear so-and-so,
> I am writing to urge your introduction of legislation in the 2015 state legislative session to ensure accountability and transparency for sexual assault victims in your state who seek a simple answer to the question that haunted me for years . . . has my rape kit been tested?
>
> When I was twenty years old, I was kidnapped while walking home to my apartment in New York City. A stranger violently robbed and raped me at gunpoint. The medical team at the hospital took great care collecting the evidence necessary to find my perpetrator. It was a grueling exam lasting several hours, its very personal nature leaving me feeling violated all over again. But I had to make sure this monster did not get away with it. I felt I owed it to myself and to society to cooperate with this invasive forensic search. Little did I realize that my rape kit, along with 17,000 others from throughout the city, would sit forgotten in police evidence rooms—untested for 9½ years. When my kit was finally tested, the evidence yielded a full DNA profile of my attacker. And a little over three years later—exactly 14 long years to the day I was attacked—the man who threatened to end my life

was finally identified in the DNA database as a serial offender. He is now in prison until 2057.

Many states have taken extraordinary measures to ensure that backlogs of unsubmitted kits are tested—passing laws for statewide audits and mandatory submission deadlines for sexual assault evidence kits. However, without a system to audit compliance, there is no way to ensure meaningful implementation of these reforms. No way to ensure that victims are kept informed, and that old backlogs of untested kits will not redevelop in the future. The solution is rape kit tracking. In fact, Congress has appropriated special funds to assist jurisdictions in developing comprehensive and collaborative approaches to addressing this issue, and has specifically included the establishment of rape kit tracking systems as a grant purpose area. Information systems for rape evidence accountability will insert transparency into the system and can be accomplished today with minimal burden.

I urge you to please consider enacting legislation to require statewide tracking of sexual assault evidence kits. I stand ready to help you in any way that I can with additional testimony and outreach.

Sincerely,

Natasha Alexenko

This is the letter I use, and it truly has had an impact. Once alerted to the issue, most elected officials have been open to rape kit reform legislation. I typically send out letters twice a year, urging them to consider supporting victims and communities in this manner. I get replies every time. Sometimes they want to move forward immediately; other times they ask that we wait another year until a new budget comes out.

I rarely get a "Thanks, but no thanks" response. I encourage anyone interested in this issue to do it—writing a letter to your representative is a good place to start.

The more seriously I was taken as a colleague, the harder I worked. Being involved in this part of the process has been so fulfilling for me both professionally and personally. I get to see the behind-the-scenes work on how legislative dreams become a reality. There were months where I was away more than I was at home, speaking at various seminars across the country. The world of rape kit reform is such a small world, and I would run into the same people over and over again—like a minireunion. This small-world aspect has its benefits, like getting to hang out with people I really like. But there are drawbacks, like the fact that few new people with new perspectives are being brought into the fold. I was so frustrated one day that I blogged about it:

> I had the opportunity to attend a hearing on the rape kit backlog. I am always inspired to hear Debbie Smith tell her story. She has this amazing ability to be articulate and chilling at the same time. I can't explain in words how effective her testimony was. Debbie brought the container that held the evidence collected from her rape kit. I won't be able to explain it nearly as well as she did so I won't even try here.
>
> Advocates from RAINN and Joyful Heart Foundation also spoke, armed with a plethora of information and statistics that were hard to ignore. I think anyone in attendance with an ounce of common sense would be moved to sign any bill and put any money necessary towards clearing the backlog of unprocessed rape kits.
>
> Unfortunately, I think we are left with that old adage of "preaching to the choir." I see the same politicians, advocates, and survivors fighting. No one new is entering this sphere. It's a tiny community! I knew about 90% of the people in

attendance. I've only been in this field for a short time, so can you imagine—I know almost everyone in this space? It always feels like a family reunion of sorts, going to these types of events. On a personal level, I enjoy that but . . .

We need more people fighting. We need new voices. How do we encourage new politicians and advocates to come on board? Everyone has been shouting at the top of their lungs, and I am certain they are exhausted.

Worth mentioning is the fact that one of the advocates at the hearing cashed in her business class train ticket so that I could take the train instead of the bus back to New York from D.C. Who does that? I'm so humbled.

We needed new people to help move our mission. We needed new people from all realms to combine their efforts in a multidisciplinary team approach. Meanwhile, RKAP helped pass laws aimed at inventorying and expediting the testing of unprocessed rape kits in twenty-two states across the nation. With me and two amazing women from two big national organizations that often collaborate to good effect, what could go wrong? A lot, apparently. There's no need for details here, and I wouldn't want internal conflict to overshadow all the progress we made. I will say that Ilse and Becca really cared about our mission, but interorganizational drama got in the way at times. It was hard for me to witness two brilliant people with such superb intentions getting off track. Often I felt like I was caught in the middle, though no one ever insisted I take sides. I was able to remain neutral most of the time, but every now and then I did weigh in.

Eventually, things went from bad to worse, and we decided to call off RKAP. I was sad, but still proud of all we'd accomplished during its two-year tenure. We'd passed legislation and brought survivors together for a summit. If you want to know where your state is in the process, look at the Appendices and check out everykitcounts.org and endthe-backlog.org.

I continued the work of Natasha's Justice Project alone, but with help from an unusual source. I'd met Lisa Hurst in 2011 at my very first DNA conference in San Diego, California. She has been my go-to expert ever since. Lisa's a lobbyist who works to push rape kit reform measures on behalf of her clients, who happen to make the instruments and chemicals used to test DNA. That may sound a little sketchy—a lobbyist with clients who benefit financially from the use and testing of rape kits. I can tell you, if all lobbyists were like Lisa, perhaps they wouldn't have such a bad reputation. That is not to say Lisa isn't fierce; she'll pounce on you before you even see her coming. She takes care of business, not waiting for anyone who isn't moving at light speed. I've met lobbyists who work around this issue and perhaps don't serve the best interests of victims. Truthfully, Lisa isn't one of them. And, for the record, I've never received a dime from Lisa or her firm (she's treated me to dinner, though, more times than I can count!).

Here's why she and I teamed up in 2014: Lisa's clients wanted to know what states were passing laws that mandate rape kit cataloguing and processing across the country. Need to know if Ohio has a law for rape kit reform on the books? Call Lisa Hurst. She'll not only know if there's a bill moving forward, she'll tell you straight-out if it sucks. With her help, I can make my case to people whom I might not normally have access to, people who have clout when it comes to legislation.

In August of 2016, I was invited to speak at the National Sexual Assault Conference, hosted by the very people who would be responsible for handing out the $80 million in grant funding—the Department of Justice. I was excited; I always love to attend events in D.C. My colleagues from RAINN and Joyful Heart Foundation were in attendance, along with law enforcement officials and lab directors I had begun to think of as friends. Just before I stepped onto the dais, I looked down at the picture on my phone that served as its screensaver: Scott and Piper asleep together on the recliner. I took a deep breath.

I'd decided to drive from New York to D.C. for the conference, thinking the trip would give me an opportunity to catch up on my podcasts. My chronic fear of bridges had reared its ugly head, and by the third large suspension bridge, I thought I was going to have a heart attack. My knuckles had turned white from clutching the steering wheel so tightly. My breathing exercises had been of no help whatsoever.

Behind the podium, with the lights in my eyes and the audience cast in shadow, I shared my harrowing driving experience. The room was full of people from every major federal bureau in the country—a group I would never have dreamed of speaking in front of.

"Surviving is a lifelong ordeal," I told them, "and I have made peace with the fact that I may have symptoms for the rest of my life."

I had finally got an idea of where my gephyrophobia came from, and I wanted to talk about it for the first time in front of this group. A week earlier, I'd been in the middle of my usual nightmare, with driving over an enormous bridge as its central theme. Except this time, when I got to the center, the bridge turned into the seventh floor of my New York apartment building. The bridge railings fell away to reveal stair railings. The water under the bridge became the staircase that had spiraled beneath me while I was being assaulted. It didn't take someone with a psych degree to figure out the meaning of that dream.

Once I got the victim narrative out of the way, I made my appeal.

"Survivors are not here to serve as the tearjerkers. We don't want to tell our stories and then be told to sit down. We are intelligent, passionate experts on this topic, and we are so much more than the stories that brought us here. We want to be more than entertainment—we want a seat at the table."

Change, especially on a systemic level, takes a long time to happen, no matter how hard changemakers are working. I had been fighting to bring attention to the issue of unprocessed kits since 2011. Finally, in 2016, I was at a place in my journey where opportunities were plentiful. My finances, however, continued to be in a state of scarcity. I thought that was just the way it is, that it would be selfish of me to feel fulfilled in what I was doing *and* not have to worry about how our next round of bills would get paid. I couldn't have both, could I? I had forgotten what it was like to not struggle to survive day to day. Scott worked hard, bless his heart, but with the expense of living on Long Island . . . it just wasn't enough.

When I first entered the world of rape kits, DNA, and lawmaking, I had a tendency to puff out my chest a bit and refuse to budge on any issue. To be honest, the underlying reason for this was that I was intimidated by the experts around me. At the same time, I was well aware how fortunate I was to be able to get to know these experts on a personal level. And once I dropped the ego and openly acknowledged my lack of academic or professional training, people began to accept me as a colleague and partner.

Patricia A. Milton is a senior research forensic scientist whom I often ran into at events across the country. Pattie has a ton of energy, and you cannot possibly keep from smiling in her presence. She began inviting me to speak at events like the Sexual Assault Kit Initiative (SAKI) National Conference, and whenever I gave the keynote, Pattie would always be there.

What I didn't realize, as I was traveling and speaking at any conference that would have me, was that my newfound friends were conspiring with Pattie to bring me onto the SAKI team as a paid consultant.

Representative Tina Orwall (with whom I had sung karaoke at the Detroit Sexual Assault Kit Summit in Michigan) was telling people that a survivor's voice was needed on the SAKI team. Ilse Knecht and Rebecca O'Connor were telling Pattie that they would appreciate having me on board. Other colleagues, like Nancy O'Malley, Dr. Rebecca Campbell, and Debi Cain from Michigan, were fighting for me behind the scenes so that I could fight alongside them. This was all done without my knowledge, with nothing but altruism and commitment to the issue driving their agenda.

After the SAKI National Meeting in June of 2016, Pattie pulled me aside. I had just completed participating on a panel alongside Dr. Campbell, and I was feeling hyped. I welcomed Pattie's exuberance.

"I'm working on getting you on the team. We need you. We want you. There's a lot of paperwork involved, so be patient. Keep texting me to check in. And you'll get paid for all the work you are doing!" she said quickly, then gave me a warm hug.

True to her word, Pattie e-mailed me at regular intervals to tell me the status of my consultant agreement, even if it was just to say "hang in there."

Then, out of the blue, I received an e-mail with a three-year consultant contract attached. I was elated. While I hadn't doubted Pattie's dedication, after so many stalled or empty or unrealized promises in the past, I just assumed things wouldn't work out. Instead, the organizers of SAKI had officially requested that I serve as a consultant to help train law enforcement officials, prosecutors, and rape crisis center staff across the nation. And, yes, this would involve a paycheck.

When they offered to pay for my services, I nearly passed out. My dream was about to be realized—a survivor of rape, with all her flaws and fears and demons, was about to work alongside those in the Department of Justice and the National Institute of Justice.

People like Pattie give me the motivation I need to keep moving forward. No matter how busy she is, she always takes a second to shoot me a quick smiley-face e-mail to let me know she's thinking about me. Always included in her communications with me is something like "Don't forget to submit your hours so you can get paid!"

Now not only do I get to do work that I am inspired by and passionate about, I don't have to subsist on ten-cent hot dogs while doing it. Every day brings a new opportunity to share and grow. And it's been quite a journey. I find myself in a good place most of the time, finding solace in the work I do. I have my moments of pain and fear, however. I spent all those years blaming myself for not catching the man that raped me sooner. I didn't think I was good enough, or strong enough. As it relates to my case, I no longer have that paralyzing fear. Now I find myself questioning whether I am worthy enough to have a podium and control of a microphone. I see so many men and women whose voices will never be heard, who still have not found a friendly ear.

I wish I could say that I am upbeat and working hard all the time. That is certainly not the case. Like most people, I have days when it's difficult to get out of bed, when I'd so much rather get lost in a video game or dive under the covers with my dog. Constantly pressing forward can be frustrating and painful, and sometimes I just want to give up.

But, most of the time, I manage. And when I emerge from whatever funk I've found myself in, I am always rewarded with something fantastic, whether it's meeting a person with new perspectives to share or discovering a new task I can sink my teeth into. Often I watch Piper frolic with the other dogs at the park. She's just so excited about everything around her, present to every moment, and unconditionally loving. My mother also continues to be a source of inspiration for me. I think of everything she went through, and everything her mother went through, and I realize that I am a link in this chain of strong, resilient women. And that I am responsible for putting the strengths I've inherited from them to good use.

The biggest driving force for me is my in-box—I am reminded of the importance of this project every time I receive an e-mail from a survivor who feels lost and alone. Thankfully, survivors across the nation have each other to lean on. To celebrate our recent victories and ensure we have more, we created a formal group of our own, tentatively called Sexual Assault Survivors Action Project (SASAP). I know that this is just the beginning of something meaningful, world-changing, and magical.

In August of 2016 Kim married her longtime partner, Vish, in Bilbao, Spain. Kim had called me months earlier to invite me to the celebration. Knowing this was a luxury I couldn't afford, she offered to pay for my trip. Not only that, but rather than accept gifts, the couple asked guests to donate to Natasha's Justice Project. I couldn't believe it.

I invited my high school friend Tanya Bhandari along for the trip to Kim's wedding. Tanya still lived in St. Catharines and would often go out of her way to check on my mother when I couldn't get ahold of her (my mother refuses to carry a cell phone!). Tanya travels all over the globe for her job, and I knew I'd be in safe hands with someone who knew their way around an airport or two.

Thanks to the many frequent-flier miles Tanya had accumulated, we flew first class across the Atlantic Ocean, each in our own little pod. I tried my best to act like this was just a normal thing I did every day, like I had never been broke or, god forbid, unable to afford to pay my electric bill! But my face gave me away—I'm sure Tanya was embarrassed by my overly childlike delight at all the extravagancies.

We landed in Bordeaux, France, and took a train to San Sebastián, Spain. As Tanya stared out the window I was struck by how beautiful she was: her long black hair, almost purple in the sunlight, a sharp contrast to my blonde curly locks and pale skin.

The hotel in San Sebastián was breathtaking. With its marble floors, wrought iron balconies, and nineteenth-century charm, I could imagine passing Queen Isabella II or Mata Hari—both had visited the city—in the lobby. We retired to our room, which had an amazing view of the bustling promenade below and the turquoise water of La Bahía de la Concha.

Throughout our travels, we had talked about the backlog and the unprocessed kits. I knew that the United Kingdom had one of the most sophisticated crime labs in the world. There, one in five women aged sixteen to fifty-nine has experienced some form of sexual violence since turning sixteen.[34] Police are required to turn in crime scene DNA to the lab within four days, and 80 percent of the time the DNA is processed and uploaded to their National DNA Database within three days. There are over 25,000 matches between perpetrators and DNA per year, and they have no backlog or unprocessed rape kits to speak of. *What's going on here in Spain?* I wondered.

As Tanya and I joined the wedding guests on a pub-hopping tour of the region, we met many locals, and I became determined to at least attempt to speak with them in Basque, throwing in a little Spanish and French where I could. Over amazing food and wine, we made conversation, and inevitably I would be asked about what I did in America. Under other circumstances I might be hesitant to talk about it, but, perhaps with the help of another elegant pour, I opened up about my work and shared the story of my project and all the neglected rape kits back at home. "Yes," I'd say, "I was raped." (I later learned that Spain has one of the lowest rates of sexual assault in Europe, with one in five[35] women experiencing it in her lifetime, very much like the United States.) The rate of reporting rape is very low, which may very well be the reason the documented sexual assault rates are so low. Our cultures may be different, but my candidness seemed to inspire theirs, and many women shared their stories with me. It might seem odd that I would travel thousands of miles and wind up talking about sexual assault, but it sort of happened organically. Suddenly we were sitting

34. "Statistics," Rape Crisis England & Wales, accessed July 27, 2017, https://rapecrisis.org.uk/statistics.php.

35. George Mills, "One in five Spanish women victim of assault," The Locales, March 5, 2014, http://www.thelocal.es/20140305/women-still-silent-on-sexual-abuse-report.

among groups of women drinking wine and struggling to describe their experiences in English. That it was a foreign tongue for most of them didn't matter in the end, as we all understood one another perfectly. Sometimes just looking into another's eyes is enough to show them you are on their side.

Kim and Vish's wedding was beyond beautiful, not because it was fancy (guests sat on hay bales during the vineyard ceremony) but because it was fun and full of love. I returned home with a renewed sense of connection to and hope for the world. I also brought home with me a new sense of urgency. Slowly but surely the rape kit backlog in the United States is being cleared, and other countries around the world have taken the lead or are following suit. I look forward to the day when no rape kits sit on shelves, when the timely testing and cataloguing of DNA is simply standard protocol, when more people will think twice before committing this terrible crime because, if nothing else, there's a higher chance that they'll get caught. Maybe this will lead to the number of rapes and assaults significantly declining—I would love nothing more than to dismantle Natasha's Justice Project because its efforts are no longer needed.

Of course, that won't be the end of it. I'd much prefer that there were no rape kits on shelves because there were no rapes, that we lived in a world where wealth was evenly distributed, where medical care and education were accessible to all, where war was a distant memory, where all people had equal rights regardless of gender, where each individual's body was not just respected but loved. Until then, we have some work to do.

ACKNOWLEDGMENTS

First and foremost, I want to give my deepest gratitude to the survivors I have met along this entire journey. I can't begin to express how essential you have been in my healing. The person I am today would not exist if it were not for you. I hope you know what you mean to me. I carry you all in my heart every day, and I want the world to know how strong and beautiful you all are.

I also want to thank Erin Calligan Mooney from Amazon for her unbelievable patience with me through the writing process! Your kindness won't be forgotten. Your dedication to survivors should be celebrated.

Joyful Heart Foundation and RAINN are two huge agencies that have taken me under their wings through the years. Ilse and Becca—you two are shining beacons to me. We may not always agree but your hearts are bigger than anyone will ever know.

Grace Freedson—the best literary agent in the world. Thank you for believing in me.

Patty Melton from the SAKI project is my dear friend, a brilliant scientist and a special human being. The world is a better place with you in it. I aspire to be more like you on a daily basis.

Jason Chin, assistant district attorney in Alameda County, and the nicest human being I know. He's put many offenders behind bars—I can't imagine what it's like to be on his bad side. Hearing stories about your beautiful family always puts a smile on my face.

My family couldn't be better if I had chosen them myself. It goes without saying that this book is an homage to my mother, Nevart. My amazing sister, Kathryn, and brilliant nephew, Alexander, have played such a huge role in this journey. My loving partner, Scott, and my extended family, the Sessas and Santa Lucias, have welcomed me with such open arms and understanding that I can hardly contain my love for them.

The amazing people I list below are not only experts in their chosen professions—they are my friends and mentors. One of the most challenging things about advocacy work is feeling as though it's you against the world. I certainly do not feel that is the case. Collectively, these amazing people make certain I am well informed, accepted in the field, and sane! I care about them both personally and professionally more than I can ever convey. I think because I share my story so openly, my relationships with those close to me tend to be wide open and honest.

I have learned a great deal about DNA, women's issues, and the human spirit. There are days when I wake up and I can hardly believe I am fortunate enough to have people standing by me and, often, standing for me. I assure you, this is the absolute and honest truth as I know it: kindness and altruism are real.

My family keeps growing all the time. I continue to meet amazing human beings on this journey, and I could fill a book just with all the ways they make me a better person. I cannot even begin to express my gratitude for these people and all the hard work they do. Sometimes, thinking about them and all of our combined accomplishments, I feel as though my heart may burst.

Debi Cain

Debi Cain is the executive director of the Michigan Domestic and Sexual Violence Prevention and Treatment Board. She is one of my most treasured friends. Debi has spent her career helping those in need.

She has inspired others through writing articles and creating curriculum for judges, police, and Child Protective Services.

Rebecca Campbell, PhD

Dr. Rebecca Campbell is a professor of psychology at Michigan State University and has been conducting community-based research on violence against women and children, with an emphasis on sexual assault, for nearly twenty-five years. Dr. Campbell and I often partner on presentations across the country. She uses her expertise on the neurobiology of trauma to communicate to law enforcement precisely how sexual assault affects a victim's ability to recall the events around the crime. Her research has shattered conventional beliefs on how victims react (or don't react) to trauma. Dr. Campbell's work exposed to us that many rapes were listed as false reports if the victim wasn't in tears when she reported the crime.

Nicole Denson

Nicole Denson is currently working as the associate director of advocacy services for Wayne County Sexual Assault Forensic Examiner's Program (WCSAFE). Her areas of expertise include crisis intervention, working with crime victims and survivors of trauma and human trafficking. Nicole has over ten years of experience working with survivors of sexual assault and domestic violence, with an extensive background working within the criminal justice system. She has helped create systems of change and activism within Michigan State University's campus, Oakland County police stations and courts, the Detroit Police Department, the 36th District Court in Detroit, the Third Judicial Circuit Court, Wayne County Prosecutor's Office, and the Frank Murphy Hall of Justice. Nicole is currently a member of the Wayne County Sexual Assault Task Force where she provides feedback on survivor-centered practices, assists in developing protocols, and participates directly in victim notifications. Nicole's passion includes advocating for equal rights for trauma survivors, women, children, and the LGBTQ community.

Amy Dowd, LMSW

Amy Dowd is currently the director of advocacy services for the Wayne County Sexual Assault Forensic Examiner's Program (WCSAFE). Utilizing cross-collaborative partnerships and a trauma-informed approach, Amy has had a rich career in the nonprofit sector. She has developed programming for emerging programs and has over fourteen years of experience providing direct services to trauma survivors, particularly those whose lives have been impacted by domestic and sexual violence. Amy has been an advising member to several groundbreaking projects in the city of Detroit, including the National Institute of Justice's Rape Kit Action Project and the Wayne County Sexual Assault Task Force. Following the discovery of over 11,000 rape kits in Detroit Police Department property storage, Amy joined local partners to assess the needs of these cases and provided assistance to those survivors whose kits had never been submitted for testing. Fighting for victim-centered practice and protocols, Amy helped to inform the research team and guide best practice recommendations for victims' rights and case notifications.

Mary DuFour Morrow

Mary DuFour Morrow is an attorney with the Prosecuting Attorneys Association of Michigan and project director for the Michigan State Police Sexual Assault Kit Initiative. As the statewide SAKI project director, she is responsible for coordinating and implementing the statewide inventory of all unsubmitted sexual assault kits, tracking testing outcomes—including the investigation and adjudication of all evidentiary leads identified through testing—and providing training to those jurisdictions dealing with large numbers of unsubmitted kits. Prior to joining the Prosecuting Attorneys Association, Morrow was an assistant prosecuting attorney with the Wayne County Prosecutor's Office and the project director for the three-year National Institute of Justice Sexual Assault Kit Initiative which examined over 11,000 sexual assault kits found in Detroit Police Department property storage.

Kimberly Hurst, PA-C

Kimberly is the founder and executive director of the Wayne County Sexual Assault Forensic Examiner's Program (WCSAFE) and a certified physician assistant. Kimberly has extensive experience at the local, state, and federal levels in improving protocols and services for sexual assault survivors in all communities. She is a sought-after speaker on the topic of sexual assault and provides healthcare providers, law enforcement officials, prosecutors, and other advocacy organizations with imperative training on how to respond compassionately and effectively to sexual assault survivors. In addition, Kimberly has been an integral part of helping to solve the issue of unsubmitted kits in Detroit.

Ilse Knecht

Ilse Knecht is the director of policy and advocacy for the Joyful Heart Foundation, one of the nation's leading organizations working toward comprehensive rape kit reform. She is recognized across the country as an expert on ways to maximize the potential of DNA technology to solve and prevent crime. For the past sixteen years, she has worked at the National Center for Victims of Crime in the public policy department and has long served as director for the National Center's DNA Resource Center. She was the project director for a three-year Office on Violence against Women Training and Technical Assistance grant to ensure a victim-centered response to the problem of back-logged and untested sexual assault kits. As part of this project, Ms. Knecht hosted more than twelve webinars, organized trainings, and created resources for the field. She authored several brochures about the use of DNA in the criminal justice system, including a brochure for victims and one for advocates and law enforcement. She has served on several advisory committees for projects related to sexual assault, forensic exams, and sexual assault response teams and has spoken extensively in the media about these issues.

Brett Kyker

Brett Kyker is an assistant prosecuting attorney in the Criminal Division of the Cuyahoga County Prosecutor's Office. Since joining the office in June of 2004, he has worked in several units including the Juvenile Justice Unit, the General Felony Unit, the Major Trial Unit, and the Internet Crimes against Children (ICAC) Unit. In December of 2014, Kyker took over as project manager of the Cuyahoga County Sexual Assault Kit Task Force. The Sexual Assault Kit Task Force is a team composed of investigators, law enforcement officers, assistant prosecuting attorneys, and victim advocates who have been assembled to address a backlog of untested sexual assault kits and prosecute offenders for sexual assaults dating back to the early 1990s.

Susan Lehman

Susan Lehman was hired as the Sexual Assault Kit Program coordinator in the Sex Crimes Unit in Portland, Oregon, in October 2015. She started her career with the Portland Police Bureau in May 1994 as a police records specialist. In January 2010, she received a promotion to police records training coordinator. Although she enjoyed her time in the Records Division, in March 2011 she was promoted to a victim assistance specialist in the Sex Crimes Unit. During this time she was instrumental in the 2014 sexual assault kit audit. Susan received an achievement award for her work as an advocate in the Sex Crimes Unit in June 2016.

Rachel Lovell, PhD

Dr. Rachel Lovell is a sociologist and methodologist who studies gender-based violence and victimization, in particular sexual assault, human sex trafficking and sex work, and intimate partner violence. Her current research involves examining issues pertaining to the unsubmitted sexual assault kits in Cuyahoga County, Ohio, and specialized dockets for human trafficking victims. She is a senior research associate at the Begun Center for Violence Prevention Research and Education at the Jack, Joseph and Morton Mandel School of Applied Social Sciences at Case Western Reserve University in Cleveland, Ohio.

James Markey

Jim Markey served for thirty years with the Phoenix Police Department, retiring in 2012 as a detective/sergeant. For fourteen years, he supervised the Sex Crime Unit. As a subject matter expert on DNA evidence in sex crimes, he has lectured nationally on using DNA in sexual assault cases. He is a member of the Arizona Forensic Advisory Committee and consults with law enforcement agencies nationwide on investigating cold case sexual assaults. He has worked locally with police agencies to develop offender DNA databases and policies on the collection of DNA evidence. Sergeant Markey collaborated with the National Institute of Justice (NIJ) National Forensic Sciences Technology Center on the use of DNA in addressing evidence backlogs and cold cases. In 2000, he developed and supervised one of the first cold case sexual assault teams. The team was nationally recognized for its achievements by the Alliance of Local Social Organizations as a Violence against Women Act success story. His eleven years of training and instructing experience include working with the National SANE/SART Conference to help create and instruct several training modules. Sergeant Markey has developed a pilot project addressing sex crime evidence backlog for the NIJ and the Executive Office of the Vice President of the United States.

Jenifer Markowitz, ND, RN, WHNP-BC, SANE-A

Dr. Jenifer Markowitz is a forensic nursing consultant who specializes in issues related to sexual assault and domestic violence, including medical-forensic examinations and professional education and curriculum development. In addition to teaching at workshops and conferences around the world, she provides expert testimony, case consultation, and technical assistance, and develops training materials, resources, and publications. Much of her work can be found on her website, Forensic Healthcare Online. Until December of 2012 she served as the medical advisor for AEquitas: The Prosecutor's Resource on Violence Against Women. A forensic nurse examiner since 1995, Dr. Markowitz served as president of the International Association of Forensics Nurses in 2012. She is board certified as a women's health nurse practitioner and as a sexual assault nurse examiner (adult/adolescent).

Jason Marzette

Jason Marzette currently works as a detective for the Wayne County Prosecutor's Office, assigned to the Sexual Assault Kit Task Force

(WCSAKTF). Detective Marzette retired after twenty-six years with the Detroit Police Department. He spent fifteen years in the Criminal Investigative Division—eight years specializing in violent crimes, four years in cybercrimes, and three years in general assignments. Detective Marzette was also an instructor with the Detroit Police Detective School.

Maria Miller

Maria Miller began her career in the Wayne County Prosecutor's Office as an assistant prosecutor assigned to the Trial Division. She has been on special assignment in the Prosecutor's Repeat Offender's Bureau (PROB), the Child and Family Abuse Bureau (CFAB), and the Special Investigations Division of the Wayne County Prosecutor's Office. In 2004, Ms. Miller became the director of communications. In this capacity, she serves as a liaison to the press, coordinates media-related projects, and receives special assignments from Prosecutor Kym L. Worthy. Ms. Miller currently serves on the State Bar of Michigan Committee for Character and Fitness as State Bar Counsel. She has been a special assistant United States attorney for the Eastern District of Michigan, a faculty member for the Prosecuting Attorneys Coordinating Council of Michigan, and a guest lecturer at the University of Michigan Law School and Wayne State University Medical School.

Lore A. Rogers

Lore Rogers is a staff attorney with the State of Michigan Domestic and Sexual Violence Prevention and Treatment Board. Previously, she worked as the interim co-director of the Sexual Assault Prevention and Awareness Center at the University of Michigan, as the director of the Domestic Violence and Sexual Assault Services Program at the

YWCA of Greater Flint in Michigan, and as the legal advocacy director at Domestic Violence Project, Inc./SAFE House in Washtenaw County, Michigan. Lore also worked as a domestic violence grant coordinator and pretrial probation compliance officer with the Washtenaw County Trial Courts. She has designed and conducted trainings on the nature and prevalence of domestic violence, domestic violence laws, law enforcement response to sexual assault, confidentiality and safety, personal protection orders, effective interviewing and assessment of survivors and batterers, working with survivors of domestic violence in family law proceedings, and the impact of domestic violence on children. Lore also has done extensive work on projects addressing unsubmitted sexual assault kits in Michigan and pilot tracking projects for these kits. Additionally, Lore has served as faculty at state and national conferences on domestic violence or sexual assault.

Taylor C. Scott

Taylor C. Scott is a CODIS Auditor at the FBI Laboratory and has been an active CODIS user/administrator since 1992. Mr. Scott worked for the Illinois State Police Forensic Sciences Command for more than 30 years as a forensic scientist. From 1992 through 2015, he was a qualified DNA analyst with their DNA databasing laboratory. In addition to being an analyst, he has held positions as CODIS administrator, technical leader, and acting assistant laboratory director. Mr. Scott has been active in DNA research on the national level through participation in the Scientific Working Group on DNA Analysis Methods (SWGDAM), National DNA Index System (NDIS) Procedures Board, and the National Institute of Standards and Technology (NIST) Organization of Scientific Area Committees for Forensic Science.

Dewanna Smith

Dewanna Smith is coordinator of the Memphis Sexual Assault Kit Task Force. She was the director of communications for former Memphis Mayor A. C. Wharton Jr. and has been a member of the SAK Task Force since its inception. She is a communications strategist with more than twenty-five years of experience in print and broadcast journalism, public relations, corporate executive communication counsel and leadership coaching, employee communications, marketing, branding, and project management.

Amy Somers

Amy Somers is an assistant prosecuting attorney in the Appellate Division of the Wayne County Prosecutor's Office, specially assigned to handle Sexual Assault Kit (SAK) cases. In addition to her appellate work, Ms. Somers regularly advises SAK prosecutors regarding the unique issues that arise in their cases, from the warrant stage through trial and sentencing. Prior to joining the Appellate Division, Ms. Somers was assigned to the District Court, Juvenile, and General Trials Divisions. She has tried hundreds of felony cases throughout her career. She has been an assistant prosecuting attorney for eleven years.

Kym L. Worthy

Wayne County Prosecutor Kym L. Worthy began her legal career at the Wayne County Prosecutor's Office in 1984. In 1989, she became the first African American selected by the office as a special assignment prosecutor, specializing in high-profile murder cases. In 1994, Worthy was elected to the Detroit Recorder's Court (now the Wayne County Circuit Court). On January 6, 2004, Worthy came full circle in her career and returned to the Wayne County Prosecutor's Office, this time as *the* Wayne County prosecutor, the first African American and the first female to hold the position. In the fall of 2007, the State Bar of Michigan conferred the prestigious Frank J. Kelley Distinguished Public Service Award upon her. Worthy was named one of "America's Best and Brightest" by two nationally circulated magazines, and has received over one hundred other awards and honors for her public service and community leadership.

Andrea Young

Andrea Young is a forensic scientist in the Biology Unit at the Michigan State Police Forensic Laboratory in Northville, Michigan. She performs autosomal DNA analysis, criminal paternity, Y-STR analysis, and STRmix analysis in casework. She has been a forensic biologist with the Michigan State Police for eleven years.

APPENDICES

Sexual Assault in the United States

Author's Note: These facts and figure reflect data until October 1, 2017. For real-time statistics please visit: natashasjusticeproject.org.

Every 1.5 minutes, another American is sexually assaulted.[36]

99.4 percent of rapists will never spend a day behind bars.[37]

15 percent of all victims of rape and sexual assault are children under the age of 12.

Rapists don't just strike once. They are often serial criminals,[38] and DNA is the single most effective rape prevention tool we have.

---

36. "Scope of the Problem: Statistics," RAINN, accessed July 6, 2017, https://www.rainn.org/statistics.

37. "The Criminal Justice System: Statistics," RAINN, accessed July 6, 2017, https://www.rainn.org/statistics/criminal-justice-system.

38. "Perpetrators of Sexual Violence: Statistics," RAINN, accessed July 6, 2017, https://www.rainn.org/statistics/perpetrators-sexual-violence.

Victims of sexual assault are, according to the World Health Organization, 3 times more likely to suffer from depression, 13 times more likely to abuse alcohol, 26 times more likely to abuse drugs, and 4 times more likely to contemplate suicide than someone who has never been sexually assaulted.

The Cost and Funding

Apprehending serial offenders early can prevent crimes, thereby saving approximately $12.9 billion a year in avoided medical costs, lost wages, and other tangible harms to victims and society.

SAFER: This grant provides federal support for state and local efforts to inventory, track, and report on backlogs of unsubmitted rape kits.[39]

SAKI: The Sexual Assault Kit Initiative (SAKI) provides $38 million in US Department of Justice grants to assist communities in responding to backlogs of untested rape kits.[40]

Debbie Smith DNA Backlog Grant Program: This long-standing federal grant is available to crime labs for DNA analysis (including rape kit backlogs) and capacity enhancement.[41]

---

39. "Sexual Assault Forensic Evidence-Inventory, Tracking, and Reporting Program Grant Program," National Institute of Justice, created March 13, 2017, accessed July 6, 2017, https://www.nij.gov/topics/forensics/lab-operations/Pages/safe-itr.aspx.

40. "Sexual Assault Kit Initiative (SAKI)," Bureau of Justice Assistance, accessed July 27, 2017, https://www.bja.gov/ProgramDetails.aspx?Program_ID=117.

41. The Debbie Smith DNA Backlog Grant Program, 42 U.S. Code § 14135 (2010).

New York DA Grant: In 2014, the New York County District Attorney's Office provided $35 million in a nationwide grant program to help jurisdictions throughout the country test backlogged rape kits. Testing is still underway.[42]

Rape Kit Backlog Reduction: Recent Successes

Colorado: 691 matches from 1,556 DNA profiles generated from previously unsubmitted rape kits (state law).[43]

Ohio: 4,367 matches from testing 12,000 kits (attorney general initiative).[44]

Detroit, MI: 2,616 matches from the testing of 10,000 kits, identifying 796 serial rapists (state law).

Alameda County, CA: 27 matches to 52 rape kit profiles (district attorney initiative).

42. Caspani, Maria, "Manhattan DA announces $35 mln funding for rape kit backlog," Reuters, November 12, 2014, http://www.reuters.com/article/us-new-york-sexcrimes-idUSKCN0IW2KJ20141112.
43. "Colorado – Backlog Snapshot," End the Backlog, accessed July 6, 2017, http://www.endthebacklog.org/colorado.
44. "Ohio – Backlog Snapshot," End the Backlog, accessed July 6, 2017, http://www.endthebacklog.org/ohio.

2017 BILL TRACKING LIST

RAPE KIT TRACKING AND RAPE KIT REFORM

LEGISLATION

as prepared by Gordon Thomas Honeywell Government Affairs

January 13, 2017

STATE	BILL	SPONSOR	SUMMARY	STATUS
RAPE KIT TRACKING				
AK	HB 31	Tarr (D)	Directs Department of Public Services to develop a rape kit tracking system for all law enforcement to use. Requires submission of rape kits within 18 months. Requires a one-time report.	INTRODUCED
MO	HB 578	Lichtennegger (R)	Model rape kit tracking bill. Mandatory participation for hospitals and law enforcement. Anonymous victim updates and semi-annual reports due.	INTRODUCED
SC	HB 3461	Cobb-Hunter (D)	Model rape kit tracking bill. Mandatory participation for hospitals and law enforcement. Anonymous victim updates and semi-annual reports due.	INTRODUCED

TX	HB 281	Howard (D)	Model rape kit tracking bill. Mandatory participation for hospitals and law enforcement. Anonymous victim updates.	INTRODUCED

RAPE KIT REFORM (NO SPECIFIC TRACKING LANGUAGE)

AZ	HB 2268	Syms (R)	Hospitals to notify Law Enforcement Agency (LEA) in 24 hours; LEA has 5 days to pick up, 15 days to submit to lab. Lab to analyze "as soon as practicable." Annual report to legislature.	INTRODUCED
CA	AB 41	Chiu (D)	Mandates participation in "SAFE-T"	INTRODUCED
IN	HB 1358	Errington (D)	Requires AG to develop guidelines on sex assault response for the state. LEA has 5 days to pick up; if prosecutor is notified, 72 hours to tell LEA to pick up; includes right of victims to be informed of kit status at various stages.	INTRODUCED
MD	HB 10	Conaway (D)	Makes changes to an annual reporting requirement for DNA evidence.	HEARING SCHEDULED
ME	LR 777		Uniform Rape Kit Examination Law. Draft language not available yet.	BILL DRAFT REQUESTED
NJ	AB 894	Huttle (D)	LEA to submit kits in 10 days; lab to analyze in 6 months. Requires statewide audit and submission of all old kits. Kits held for 90 days.	INTRODUCED
NJ	AB 2318	Huttle (D)	Mandatory victim notification for rape kit status.	INTRODUCED

NJ	SB 839	Pou (D)	LEA to submit kits in 10 days; lab to analyze in 6 months. Requires statewide audit and submission of all old kits. Kits held for 90 days.	INTRODUCED
NM	SB 7	McSorley (D)	Appropriates $1.2 million in FY 18 and FY 19 to local authorities for processing rape kits if the local lab can provide a match of $2 million for each year.	INTRODUCED
NV	AB 55	Judiciary	LEA to submit kit in 30 days. Labs have 180 days to test. Annual report required from lab on # of kits received and # tested.	INTRODUCED
NY	AB 375	Simotas (D)	Chapter amendment to 2016 law. Required statewide count of all untested kits in the state by Mar 1, 2017. Quarterly reports due to the legislature.	See NY SB 980
NY	SB 980	Hannon (R)	Chapter amendment to 2016 law. Required statewide count of all untested kits in the state by Mar 1, 2017. Quarterly reports due to the legislature.	PASSED SENATE, PASSED HOUSE COMMITTEE
VA	HB 2127	Levine (D)	Rights on notification to victims for destruction of anonymous kits.	INTRODUCED
VT	HB 25	Grad (D)	Right to have kit sent to lab within 72 hours of collection, and to be informed of matches or destruction.	INTRODUCED

SAMPLE LEGISLATION

STATEWIDE AUDITS OF UNSUBMITTED RAPE KITS

SECTION 1. <u>STATE LAW</u> is amended to read as follows:

(a) As used in this section:

(1) "Forensic medical examination" means an examination provided to the victim of a sex offense by a health care provider for the purpose of gathering and preserving evidence of a sexual assault for use in a court of law;

(2) "Sexual assault evidence kit" means a human biological specimen or specimens collected by a health care provider during a forensic medical examination from the alleged victim of a sex offense; and

(3) "Untested sexual assault evidence kit" means a sexual assault evidence kit that has not been submitted to the <u>STATE CRIME LAB</u> or a similar qualified laboratory for deoxyribonucleic acid (DNA) analysis.

(b) Inventory of Untested Kits.

(1) By <u>DATE</u>, all law enforcement agencies and departments charged with the maintenance, storage, and preservation of sexual assault evidence kits shall conduct an inventory of all such kits being stored by the agency or department before the effective date of this act which have not been submitted for testing. The inventory shall be transmitted to the <u>STATE AUDITOR/ATTORNEY GENERAL</u>.

(2) By <u>DATE</u>, the <u>STATE AUDITOR/ATTORNEY GENERAL</u> shall prepare and transmit a report to the speaker of the state senate and speaker of the state house of representatives containing the number of untested sexual assault evidence kits being stored by each county, by each law enforcement agency or department, the date the untested kit was collected, the corresponding statute of limitations for prosecution for the crime associated with each kit, and shall consult with the state crime laboratory on a plan for addressing the untested kits.

(c) Annual Report.

(1) All law enforcement agencies and departments charged with the maintenance, storage, and preservation of sexual assault evidence kits shall annually report untested kits in their possession to <u>STATE AUDITOR/ATTORNEY GENERAL</u> no later than <u>DATE</u>.

(2) The <u>STATE AUDITOR/ATTORNEY GENERAL</u> shall obtain numbers of untested kits the law enforcement agency or departments fail to report as required in subparagraph (1).

(3) The <u>STATE AUDITOR/ATTORNEY GENERAL</u> shall compile all of the data into an annual report that shall be posted on a publicly accessible Internet website by <u>DATE</u> of each year. The report shall also be issued to the state legislature by <u>DATE</u> of each year.

SAMPLE LEGISLATION

Reform Of Rape Kit Evidence Submission Policy

Sec. 1. DEFINITIONS—The need for definitions will vary by state and may depend on other existing laws and common practices in a state.

Sec. 2. (1) A health care facility that has obtained written consent from a person from whom a sexual assault evidence kit has been collected shall notify the law enforcement agency having jurisdiction within 24 hours after obtaining that consent to report the incident as a crime.

(2) A health care facility that has not obtained written consent to report the crime from a person from whom a sexual assault evidence kit has been collected shall inform the individual from whom sexual assault kit evidence was obtained of its sexual assault kit evidence storage and retention policy. The information shall include a statement of the period for which that evidence will be stored before it is destroyed and how the individual can have the evidence released to the investigating law enforcement agency at a later date. Any sexual assault kit evidence that is not released to a law enforcement agency under this section shall be stored for a minimum of 1 year before it is destroyed.

(NOTE: In no instance should this provision be altered to provide for less time than what is already provided under state or local policies.)

Sec. 3. (1) A law enforcement agency that receives notice under section 2 that sexual assault kit evidence has been released shall take possession of the sexual assault kit evidence from the health care facility within 7 days after receiving that notice.

(2) If a law enforcement agency determines that the alleged sexual assault occurred within the jurisdiction of another law enforcement agency and that it does not otherwise have jurisdiction over that assault, that law enforcement agency shall notify the other law enforcement agency of that fact within 7 days after receiving the kit from the health care facility that collected the sexual assault kit evidence.

(3) A law enforcement agency that receives notice under subsection (2) shall take possession of the sexual assault kit evidence from the other law enforcement agency within 7 days after receiving that notice.

(4) The investigating law enforcement agency that takes possession of any sexual assault kit evidence shall assign a criminal complaint number to that evidence in the manner required by that agency and shall submit that evidence to the state crime laboratory or another accredited laboratory for analysis within 7 days.

(5) All sexual assault kit evidence submitted to the state laboratory or an accredited laboratory on or after the effective date of this act shall be analyzed within 30 days of receipt by the state crime laboratory or other accredited laboratory.

(6) The failure of a law enforcement agency to take possession of sexual assault kit evidence as provided in this act or to submit that evidence

for analysis within the time prescribed under this act does not alter the authority of the law enforcement agency to take possession of that evidence or to submit that evidence to the state crime laboratory or other accredited laboratory and does not alter the authority of the state crime laboratory or other accredited laboratory to accept and analyze the evidence or to upload the DNA profile obtained from that evidence into state and national DNA databases.

(7) The failure to comply with the requirements of this act does not constitute grounds in any criminal proceeding for challenging the validity of a database match or of any database information, and any evidence of that DNA record shall not be excluded by a court on those grounds.

(8) A person accused or convicted of committing a crime against the victim has no standing to object to any failure to comply with the requirements of this act, and the failure to comply with the requirements of section 2 or section 3 is not grounds for setting aside the conviction or sentence.

Sec. 4. If a law enforcement agency intends to destroy or otherwise dispose of any sexual assault kit evidence in a sexual assault offense case before the expiration for the limitation period provided for prosecution, the law enforcement agency with primary responsibility for investigating the case shall notify the victim of that intention, including the reasons for the decision, in writing at least 60 days before the evidence is destroyed or otherwise disposed of.

ABOUT THE AUTHOR

Born on Long Island, New York, and raised in St. Catharines, Ontario, Canada, Natasha Simone Alexenko is the founder and CEO of Natasha's Justice Project (NJP), a national nonprofit organization created to expose and eliminate the nationwide rape kit backlog and to bring justice to survivors of sexual assault. Alexenko has been featured in the *New York Times*, the *Wall Street Journal*, and other national and international publications. She has made guest appearances on broadcast and cable networks and was the focus of the HBO documentary *Sex Crimes Unit*. Alexenko shared her story at the historic 2015 joint press conference at which Vice President Joe Biden and New York County (Manhattan)

District Attorney Cyrus Vance Jr. pledged a combined $80 million to help defray the cost and reduce the backlog of untested rape kits. Alexenko serves as a consultant to the Department of Justice Bureau of Justice Assistance's Sexual Assault Kit Initiative Grants (SAKI). For more information, visit www.NatashasJusticeProject.org.